A gripping and very moving book.
—Kim Hill, Radio New Zealand

Henry has a clear voice, a fine sense of place and an unsentimental honesty in grappling with the unwieldy matters of family, collective trauma and writing.
—Sally Blundell, *NZ Listener*

Here is all the evidence you need that good writing can make something extraordinary out of the relatively ordinary. Chessie Henry's family is remarkable in many ways, but they're not public figures or mega-achievers in any field. Through the lens of her prose, however, they assume a very impressive stature.
—Paul Little, *North & South*

This story of family is thrilling, heartbreaking, and wholeheartedly human.
—Lizzie Murray, *Wellington Regional News*

We Can Make a Life

Chessie Henry

Victoria University Press

TE WHARE WĀNANGA O TE ŪPOKO O TE IKA A MĀUI

VICTORIA
UNIVERSITY OF WELLINGTON

VICTORIA UNIVERSITY PRESS
Victoria University of Wellington
PO Box 600 Wellington
vup.victoria.ac.nz

Published with assistance from

creative
nz
ARTS COUNCIL OF NEW ZEALAND *TOI AOTEAROA*

ISBN 9781776561940

A catalogue record for this book is available from the
National Library of New Zealand.

Printed in China by 1010 Printing International

For my parents

Contents

From: *Chris Henry*
To: *Jo Scott-Jones*
Date: *17 April 2017 7:03:12 AM NZST*
Subject: *burnout*

Hi Jo,

Sorry to be asking your advice again, but I trust you to point me in the right direction.

I have been gradually sinking the last few months (with our night out in Welly a notable exception!).

I wake every night at about 3am, and for some reason decided today to write a letter—not really to anyone in particular, but referencing discussions I have had with a counsellor here.

Now I am not sure what to do with it! Have wondered about sending to my GP (not that I have a GP), or the psychiatrist I am booked to talk to—or whether just to send to a counsellor.

My more radical alter ego wants to send it to The Press or Jonathan Coleman, saying PLEASE STOP (you idiot) giving out free GP visits, and instead try supporting the exhausted Drs, nurses and admin staff, who are overwhelmed by needy patients wanting everything for nothing.

It is a bleak read, and probably inaccurate about yours and our colleagues' reasons for leaving general practice—so please excuse that—but the sentiment is very real. That said, it was 4am and I am not that low all the time. I am safe, and not about to go for a long swim, so don't worry re that.

I know you are very busy but would really value a steer as to where to go next. I need a break—as you have often told me—that at least is clear.
Chris

My letter:

It is 4am Sunday. I've been on call since Friday morning, but also had my parents staying which has, at last, brought me someone I trust enough to tell how I feel, and someone who believes and understands the sadness, frustration and despair Esther feels watching me disintegrate like an ultra slow motion car crash.

Woke earlier in panic and sweat after nightmare that started with me at a conference trying to sort out rural funding or something, ending in argument, then leaving that and becoming a race to find tickets and get to train platform to get home but losing Rufus and running back and forth in increasing panic till I woke up.

Have suddenly had a moment of clarity.

I know five very highly regarded rural GPs, my age or a bit older (four of whom have also been publicly acknowledged for their efforts, making my award feel like kiss of death).

All 5 left their practices in the last few years, only one had a nice planned retirement with the thanks and praise they deserved, and even then only just.

Final straw moments were:
- *marriage breakdown*
- *mental health issues*
- *'burnout'*
- *heart attack (attributed very much to stress)*
- *HDC investigation—so unfair and demoralising he resigned*

Any and all of those scenarios could be me right now.

Esther stands heroically beside me, but my life is consumed by work or feeling stressed by work and our relationship (and mine with the kids) teeter on the brink. I have no close friends.

As we have discussed I feel overwhelmed, anxious and

depressed. *I can see no way out of my work responsibilities and pressures, and no way forward from the emotional and financial disaster of the house we can't even visit, let alone use, rent, repair or ever sell; our most crucial emotional pillar and only financial asset is lost.*

I can't give up with work entirely—I need to weather this storm and hope to return one day if I am ever to have a business that is worth anything.

I am in the worst physical shape of my life: high BP, massive stress, heart pounding as I write this, my head hurts, my knees hurt, I'm 10kg overweight. I can't sleep and have a really awful sense of impending doom re health.

I am so behind with admin, results, letters etc. and so busy covering and advising locums, the newer doctors and the nurses that it impossible to stay on top of it all or even to know or remember what I have checked off or who I've seen. Mistakes are happening—two recent 'missed' diagnoses, complaints re late referrals etc.—I'm scared that I don't even know about what else I have missed.

Add to that a tolerance of zero and irritability—in the last few weeks I have made an embarrassing furious outburst at conference and have lost my temper with admin staff, a poor night nurse at hospital and patients. I am really worried about medicolegal risk and inevitable complaints that will grind on for years.

On Friday I had call about a long-time patient of mine who I had sent down to Christchurch earlier in week with what we thought was easily treated tumour; however turns out to be inoperable and essentially untreatable so I was told that he was coming back to 'GP care'.

I am ashamed to admit that my first thought was about how would I find the time, energy or interest for the horrible journey ahead, without a flicker of compassion.

I am not sure I can pull myself together for my acute

clinic at 10am, or for the day and night on call ahead, let alone the next few weeks or months. I was thinking in mad desperation last night of ringing John Kirwan or David Meates to say please help me, what can I do? I cannot go on.

I am frightened; I don't know which of the outcomes will get me first, but feel certain this will not end well.

Hāpuku

The road home was gravelled, loose in places and rising into mounds at either bank. It was a straight road, for the most part, clinging to the edges of a flat stretch of coastline, elevated a little way above the sea. Despite the water in plain sight it felt hot—or at least, it all seemed to evoke hotness; the tussock burnt yellow-green and dry, the charcoal-coloured sand of the beach. That day it seared, heat rising out of the ground and blurring everything, the dreaded hole in the ozone layer like a vast, invisible puncture overhead.

Old Beach Road, Hāpuku. At first our new address had appealed in an underdog kind of way—a name belonging to a beach whose beauty had been overlooked, eclipsed by whiter sand and milder water. In fact, it was the opposite, pushing people away with its burning black dunes and crashing, volatile waves. Sometimes it was so windy down there we couldn't hear ourselves talk, sand whipping our exposed legs, the sound of the waves roaring into our bedrooms at night. To stand out there on the edge of the tussock, and have it all spread out before you—it had us whooping, just to make ourselves heard against the wildness.

We weren't allowed to swim in the water. Sometimes in the summer we saw hippies going in, when the roads were busier and people drifted down to the ocean. Tourists would sit around kissing and burning, leaning their backpacks up against the rough sand. Once, a nudist—we spied him from where we were playing along the tussocked dunes, with his hands on hips and sporting a floppy sunhat, tufts of white hair down his back. He stared out across the water, and then strode in, his backside small and deflated in the midday sun. We clapped our hands across our eyes and cackled, horrified. Who would pull a naked guy out of the water if he got caught in a rip? Not us.

Running between the beach and the road was the TranzCoastal railway line, tracking its rickety course along the tracks behind our house. The trains roared past periodically, a rush of cargo or blurred faces, the coins we left out on the tracks turned flat and pictureless. We figured the noise was a small price to pay for our little home on the edge of everything, a hidden gem between the snow-covered mountains and sea. This was our house before Clarence, and before earthquakes. Years later, when we returned to Hāpuku, the road would be tar-sealed, summer heat rising from the black asphalt in a hazy mirage. But back then it was gravel, and the cars that passed were always followed by white clouds of gritty dust. The dust textured your hair if you left the windows down as you drove along—or biked, as I did that day.

I was thirteen, and I was on my way home from the purple-and-yellow dairy, a lurid legoblock building which marked the end of Old Beach Road and the meeting of the highway as it swept into Kaikōura. We were allowed to bike as far as the dairy, returning with tongues turned red from popsicle slushies and sherbet, salt and vinegar chips burning the roofs of our mouths. It was five k's back to the house. I pumped my feet up and down on the pedals, the seat hot from where I'd left the bike out in the sun, sugar singing in my veins.

I turned to look back when I heard the sirens, the familiar

shape of Dad's Land Rover humming towards me in the distance, a dust cloud in his wake. I could see the lights glittering—inside the car there was a button, a wire winding up and outside the window to where they were screwed onto the roof. He would turn them on for us sometimes when he was coming up the driveway, the siren wailing to us that he was home. I was nearly too old for it: the squealing *Dad's back!* and the race to the door, hopping our bare feet over the sharp limestone chips of the garden path.

On the side of the road, I swung my legs off my bike, ready to flag him down for a pick-up. I put one hand to my shoulder, feeling its hot burn. We always forgot to wear sunblock—my nose was hard and cracked, my arms turned dark. When I held them up against my pale stomach in the shower, it was as though they were separate from my body; a stranger's limbs.

I watched his eyes flick towards me as he sped past, forcing me to turn my back against the dust. I was still some distance from the house, and I watched him race away, the car disappearing after he crossed the one-way bridge and the road curved out of sight. 'Shit,' I said loudly, letting the expletive hang in the otherwise emptiness, the quiet left behind once the sirens had passed. I kicked my feet back on the pedals and pushed forward, irritated and thirsty. Dumb, I thought, stupid. Why didn't he stop for me?

I pedalled over the little bridge, the creek below mostly dried up, white towering flowers with their thick, aggressive stems lining the way. The stalks oozed out sap when you snapped them, milky white and sharp-smelling. Spiders laid their nests in the weeds here, creamy sacs bulging in the sun. I left it all behind, the road rising upwards—a short burst of incline followed by the steady sweep down. On the up my cheeks burned, streaks of dirt on my forearm where I'd wiped my mouth. Halfway I stopped to walk my bike, hoping no cars drove up behind me and saw. My brothers biked this stretch like it was nothing, their legs moving like water. I felt slow and hot, hair slick down the back of my neck.

On the downward slope I set off again, and as I rounded the corner I could see the Land Rover parked haphazardly in the tussock on the roadside. Its front door was open from where my father had spilled out of it. He was kneeling now, his hands working quickly over the body of a man who was lying on his back. I biked towards them slowly. There was a dune buggy on its side, and boys everywhere—lying down or sitting up, bloody. There was a quiet feeling, a buzzing, the boys silent except for a low moaning sound coming from one whose legs bent strangely out of place at the thighs. I recognised some of them—older guys, from the high school. They'd made me feel nervous, mostly, when I saw them around. A couple of times over the summer I had been to the movies in town, and they would sit at the back smelling like sweat and Lynx deodorant, shouting insults at each other and laughing, their trackpants and jackets rustling during the quiet parts. One of them had thrown a Snifter at the back of my head and I'd frozen, too afraid to turn around.

Now, I stared. One boy had pulled himself across the road to lean against a fencepost in the grass. He sat, stunned and silent, eyes set blankly towards the sea. He looked pale, his arms hanging at his sides, gravel studded across his skin.

'Dad,' I said, uncertain, still on tiptoe with my feet off the pedals. He was on his knees with his medical pack, moving calmly between the boys. He didn't answer, just looked up to smile tightly, his mind somewhere else. Blood had soaked into the gravel and was drying in the sun, dark compared with its redness on the boys' skin. There were about eight of them—more than could fit safely into the dune buggy, even I knew that. Behind them I could see tracks in the gravel, long swooping curves. One of them seemed worse than the others, quieter. He seemed to be having trouble breathing—or, in any case, Dad had set up a blue plastic breathing cup over his mouth.

I could feel heat starting to colour my cheeks, became aware of my heart beating. I wondered briefly if everyone else could hear it, if they could see the sweat prickling on the handlebars under my palms. The one with the broken legs made me feel dizzy, but really all of it did—the blue sky, the glare on the gravel and the boys' skin, so easily torn open where they'd hit the road, thrown out of the buggy like knuckle bones. Dad was making calls on his phone, talking to the boys, touching them here and here, his hands on their broken bodies like code. I stayed on my bike, wheeling myself off to the side when the ambulance showed.

I don't know when Dad appeared, but he did, clapping his hand on my elbow and squeezing me towards him. 'Well,' he said cheerfully, 'they'll all be fine. You should head home, honey. I'm relieved, I'll say that.'

He looked pale in his high-vis vest, blood streaked across his trousers where he'd wiped his hands. He could probably come home to change, I thought, because we were so close anyway. That way he wouldn't have to be bloody for the rest of the day, in front of the normal patients. 'I thought it was us, actually,' he said, nodding towards the dune buggy. 'Call out for our address, carload of boys . . . I thought for sure it was your brothers. Seems silly now. They can't even drive.' He smiled at me. I thought about him racing down the road, rushing past me, full up with the image of his four sons bruised and bleeding on the roadside.

My ride home was slow and heavy, as though I had been swimming in my clothes, my shoes filled up with water, weighing me down. As I crossed the railway line I stopped to put twenty cents on the tracks for later. We collected them, our flattened coins—long past wondering if they would derail the trains that thundered over them. The coin seemed bright against the rust-coloured rails; a tiny, silver full moon, unaware of what was coming for it—all heat and noise, unstoppable. I left it there and pedalled on, past the abandoned goat house and the mailbox, the giant tree and the pancake stones we had piled up into towers. I dumped my bike on the lawn and looked up towards the house. My mother was visible in the kitchen window, her head bent down, her back to me. I flopped down beside the bike, the wheels still spinning, and wondered vaguely when the next train would be. It felt like forever had passed since I'd left for the dairy, or hardly any time at all.

Drummond Street

I'm writing this from my bedroom in Wellington. Summer is on its way out, only the last keen swimmers left plunging into the harbour. Above, the sky is milky, swollen with rain. I have a big desk in my room, looking out over the Mount Cook stairs, but it's mostly for show—I always end up writing in bed, usually early in the morning. The window in my room is large and even from my bed I can see what's happening out on the stairs. It's a funny part of Wellington, a mix of students and professionals, young families, elderly people living on their own. The stairs are wide and lined with benches and plants, a public walkway connecting Tasman and Drummond Streets. Somehow the stairs became a stopping point for people passing by, school kids there to break up or make up, crying into the flax bushes. Or sweaty middle-aged running groups doing drills up and down, their breathless banter spilling into my room. Sometimes drunk guys, swaying on the benches. They smell like urine and booze, and they never seem to notice as I walk by. Once, two guys at the top of the stairs, high as kites and negotiating their route down in a small chilly bin. 'Don't do that,' I pleaded, watching one of them crush himself inside it. 'That will definitely kill you.'

'Aw, ya know,' he said. 'Gotta do it.'

Other times it's just people holding hands, or sliding down the handrails on the seat of their pants. Sometimes I see friends and I call out, but they don't hear me. Always there are Massey students—the university is just beyond the top of the stairs. When I was a student there I lived in a house nearby, dashing across the road five minutes before my classes, arriving pink-cheeked, half asleep.

I first arrived in Wellington off the ferry, laden with the bags that Mum and I had packed together at home. My friend picked me up and took me back to her flat in the centre of the city, just off Cuba Street. It felt like a life I hadn't even known I'd wanted until that exact minute when we were walking round her room, the walls covered with art prints and drunken, obscure messages from new friends; inky, sprawling handwriting and joke-names I'd never heard before. She lived with long-haired boys who wore ripped jeans, and I stared openly at everyone, wanting to be like them. Wellington felt like a city where you became the person you'd always imagined—or, at least, where you sat coolly at the back of bars listening to people play jazz, or something.

I started out studying English literature at Victoria University of Wellington. It was a badly planned year, organised from a grubby internet café somewhere in London during my gap year, when decisions about classes and courses had felt like distant plans for a future self, a stranger. Soon I switched to Massey and began a degree in communications. It felt more practical than studying novels, but still, at the end of those three years, the thought nagged at me: I wanted to be a writer. In 2015 I applied for the Master's in Creative Writing at Victoria's International Institute of Modern Letters. I'd heard about the course years before—the best you could do, people said, the one that would push you out of your comfort zone. When I was accepted, the email went to my junk folder, so I almost never saw it.

The idea was to write a novel over the course of a year, and the finished product would be our thesis. I sat in a room with ten other writers, paralysed with nerves. But as the months passed, a story surfaced—a work of fiction set in an alternative, future Wellington. It was about a community rebuilding after a flood.

That novel is sitting in a folder on my desktop now, needing work. It's still a good story, I think, but I'm not ready to go back to it yet. I want to write all of this down first: a different book, one that's been swimming around my head for the last couple of years. I can feel it starting to fit together – the earthquakes, Dad and his work as a doctor, the demands of rural medicine. Fractured emotions. Feeling out of control. And then, as well: the things that keep you steady.

It's different writing something true. It actually feels a little bit like cheating—I don't have to make up the plot, develop any of the characters. They're already here, fully formed in front of me, doing things that make me want to write about them. In the months leading up to the summer of the end of my MA year, I'd talked it over with my parents, asking them how they'd feel if, for my next project, I wrote about what we'd all been through. 'Would you mind?' I asked.

'We just want you to write,' they told me. 'It doesn't matter to us what you write about.'

*

It's been seven years since I arrived in Wellington, and I've become my own small part of the rhythm of the city, my adoration for it only slightly less delusional. I've come and gone in that time, chasing jobs or going overseas, home for summer holidays. But still, it's a place that always sparks that same feeling, like everything is possible again. I'm surprised it can have such a hold on me, because I am equally rooted at home—small-town New Zealand, the epic spread of mountains and sea, no cellphone reception and empty black-sand beaches. There, it doesn't matter if people read your work or not. There's no anxiety; it's just big and wild. You can't shake that stuff. I come and go between these two homes, flying to Kaikōura every few months just to breathe out, to not be chasing anything.

These are my landscapes. But now that I'm writing, I'm faced with another set: the ones that belonged to my parents in their lives before New Zealand, and before us. They've taken us kids back to England to visit, but I feel out of place there—the wrong clothes, the wrong accent. The green fields and cobbled streets don't carry any significance for me. My brothers and I joke that we are the weird hillbilly cousins, turning up once every couple of years with stories of pig hunting or mincing paua, laughing about the deranged wild goat that lives in the hills in Clarence, our impossibly remote home, tucked away along the east coast of New Zealand.

In Wellington, I sit up in bed with my laptop to write. It's strange to look back over my life like this, seeing afresh how one thing leads to another. This story goes back further than me—there is stuff that only really makes sense if you know what's gone before. But once I start travelling backwards, it seems impossible to contain everything, all these lives with their influences, events from a century ago still rippling into today. I try not to think about the process, knowing there will always be an infinite number of possible tellings. Instead, my writing is an exercise of trust—pieces rise to the surface and I gather them up, order them, assign meaning based on gut-feeling. A part of me feels nervous, backing myself like this. The more I write the more the story narrows, leaving less room to change tack. But I keep going because there's a confident part of me, too. Sometimes, when I'm working, I don't feel nervous at all.

17 July 1960

My parents were born on the exact same day: 17 July 1960. Christopher and Esther, brand new, blinking in the sudden brightness of their separate hospitals, fifty miles apart. For my entire life this fact has remained fun—I am embarrassed to find myself telling people about it whenever birthdays come up in conversation, as though I still believe it is somehow meaningful or significant. (*They are totally soulmates,* my friends say loyally.) In my own life I don't really believe in soulmates, or even in really 'knowing' a person is for you. But as a kid I was obsessed—like most kids are, I guess—with my parents' love story. Even now I feel a strange lightness when it comes up, a spark of faith in inevitability, a bizarre pride that they managed to meet.

I picture my two grandmothers, strangers to one another, young women living out their happy and not-so-happy marriages in the 1950s. Over nine months they have observed their bodies swelling, held their hands to the roundness of their bellies and felt the kicks. And now, on 17 July, here they are at the hospital. Today they have been through something monumental. They are exhausted and emotional—they have just given birth. Their newborn babies won't cross paths until they are much older, until nearly three decades have gone by, these sterile hospital rooms so far behind them.

I know the house they took Dad back to—the Old House, says the little signpost nailed to the front exterior. This is my grandparents' place, somewhere I visited as a kid once every couple of years. It always felt familiar despite the distance, twenty thousand kilometres away in Surrey, England. My father grew up in Pirbright, a quintessential English village complete with a church, pub and village hall. In the flickering film of their home movies, the grass stands out: a deep green against the pink of my grandmother's dress. She is classic and beautiful, her boys clumsy and flushed in her lap. My dad grins, holding a fish or riding a bicycle. The buttons of his brown woollen cardigan have been done up in a hurry; his hair flops over his eyes.

My dad was close to his mother, growing up. He still calls her all the time, asking her advice or telling her our news. When I was a child I would savour the hours I spent with her, begging my parents to let me wake her up, hanging off her arms and demanding attention. Granny, I call her, although her name is Lindy. We would sit around her wooden table and make jewellery, paint watercolours, craft tiny, delicate dolls from crêpe paper and clay. I often mucked them up, clumsy and overeager, but Granny could fix everything, sewing up rips with her impossible invisible stitches.

Dad was her second child of four in a rough-and-tumble world—not much money and hand-me-down clothes, little shorts tatty and faded by the time they reached youngest. When I interview her for this book, Granny laughs as she tells me about the first time they went out for dinner as a family, when my father was eight or nine years old. None of the children had ever been in a restaurant before, and she ordered every member of the family an omelette.

As a boy, Granny tells me, my father was sensitive and caring, the kind of kid who brought sick animals home on his walk back from school, or who complimented his mother's friends on their clothes. 'He's one of a kind,' they would tell her, but she already knew. My grandfather, Richard, was kind and attentive to his boys, seeking to make amends for the troubled relationship he'd had with his own father. An accountant for most of his life, in middle-age he had a change of heart and quit his office job, spending his days tinkering around in the garage. To everyone's surprise, he went on to invent a metal device that could securely fix loose screws back into wooden railway sleepers. This invention was the first of its kind, and as a child I think I always defined him as an inventor, a thinker, someone who knew everything. I would pick up his things carefully—engraved pens and heavy paperweights—my fingers leaving marks on the glossy dark wood of his desk.

In 1973 Dad left Pirbright for Radley College, a traditional English boarding school in Oxfordshire. We tease him about it—his fancy school—always calling it 'Bradley' just to wind him up. He'll correct my brother Matt's grammar, and Matt will wink at him. 'Should've sent me to Bradley, Chris!' Somewhere in my childhood it was relayed to me that at Radley, all the boys wore robes, and unfortunately in my mind the whole school has become Hogwarts. Whenever Radley comes up I have a vision of Dad striding round with his tousled black hair and green eyes, his robes billowing out behind him across the grass.

Even if he gets a hard time about it now, Radley was formative for Dad—I guess high school always is, in one way or another. It started in his first year. Osgood–Schlatter disease: an inflammation of the area just below the knee, where the tendon from the kneecap attaches to the shinbone. It's a common problem for boys doing a lot of exercise. Now, Dad tells me, it would most likely be treated by telling someone just to get on with it. But back then, it was a disaster: an operation on both knees, no more sports. Compulsory school sport took up every afternoon, so my father was left aimless, confined to casts and solitude while his friends carried on without him. He hung around in the metalwork department after school, the teacher taking pity on him and letting him tinker. He learnt how to put things together and take them apart, absorbing himself in the tasks set for him, the whirring quiet of the empty classroom.

Dad's geography teacher was a Scottish man called John Wiley, and when he discovered my father's newfound freedom he tracked him down, adamant that they should start a sailing club. They made the boats from scratch—even the fibreglass hulls—John lecturing Dad on Scottish history while they worked. By the time they had their little fleet they had also recruited more boys, taking the boats out to a flooded quarry nearby, gradually getting their heads around the intricacies of sailing.

Dad could no longer play rugby with his injured knees, but he could swim. He took up scuba diving, training in the frigid waters of the school pool, later becoming affiliated with the Oxford Dive Club, where his fellow goose-bumped, adolescent teammates would travel to do their tests. Like building things, diving required quiet focus, the watery hum underneath the surface pool wholly encompassing. Soon Dad's days were full again, building and sailing and diving, returning to his little cubicle room at night with aching muscles and ears full of water.

*

Try as I might, I can't seem to shed entirely my parents' voices in this retelling. And more than that, I wasn't there; the 'whirring quiet of the empty classroom' is a sound I imagine belonging to a room I've never visited.

I first heard the word 'sentimental' used in reference to writing during my Master's year. I hadn't put the two together before then. I'd thought about 'emotive' or 'nostalgic' writing, maybe. But 'sentimental' was different. I felt a grim kind of sinking feeling, and returned to my room that night to google *sentimentality*. 'Exaggerated and self-indulgent tenderness, sadness, or nostalgia,' the dictionary spat back at me. Oh god, I remember thinking. This is me, my work. *Self-indulgent tenderness*. Could anything be worse?

I spent the following weeks trying to cleanse all my work of sentimentality. Anything that felt tender was deleted. Then, with a horrible sick feeling, I suddenly remembered my blog, which had *poetry* on it. And it was up there, on the internet. I had put it there myself, in the carefree days before sentimentality was a thing I knew about. I spent the next ten minutes trying to remove it, eventually locating the 'deactive live' button. I felt so flooded with relief I had to lie down.

'But,' my boyfriend said a few weeks later, when I was still thinking about it, 'isn't that . . . just who you are, a bit?'

'*What?*' I squeaked back. 'Self-indulgent? Over the top?'

'No!' he said nervously. 'I meant, like, you always write from your heart, sort of thing.' He sighed. 'I don't mean . . . don't worry.'

I'm still not sure what my relationship is to sentimentality. I better understand what is meant by it, perhaps—that sentimental writing is work that is oversimplified, overly fond, designed for an easy tug at readers' heartstrings. But a large part of me also feels defensive of sentimentality. We dismiss it so easily, and so wholly, that sometimes even the faintest sign of it will have us edging away, nervous and disparaging.

That phrase—self-indulgent—makes me nervous. Actually, they all do: tender, sad, nostalgic. I wasn't there for my parents' childhoods. But still I want to recreate them, ask my parents over and over again how it felt, what it looked like.

*

Sixty-odd miles away from Radley, my mother was in the equivalent year at St Albans High School for Girls. She would travel from home to school every day, but unlike the Old House, which is so familiar to me, I never saw the house my mother grew up in. By the time I was born her parents had separated and her childhood home was long gone. Everything I know about it has been recounted to me, my fond ideas shaped entirely by my parents' stories.

Mum's mother, Anne, was a florist. She was a devoted parent, endlessly interested in her three children and maintaining a close relationship with all of them, even as they moved into adulthood. All these years later, whenever I return home after being away, Mum will put cut flowers from the garden in a little vase beside my bed—the same as Anne did for her, like a passed-down signature. Mum's father, John, was a businessman, and then later a builder. He is the kind of man you'd call larger-than-life: rough hands, a solid frame. Back then he was always joking, playing pranks or starting trouble, like the time he and a friend had a few too many drinks on St Patrick's Day and painted all the white lines of the local zebra crossing green. He recognised the same cheeky character in my young mother, and couldn't help but nurture that side of her.

They lived in Hertfordshire, in a big old house called Manor Farm, with a pool and stables. My mother grew up well educated and well spoken—seaside holidays in Salcombe and white buckled shoes. She was the eldest, Andrew and Lucy behind her, dark-haired next to their sunny blondness. Mum was always kind and well mannered, but prone to periods of naughtiness that ran on well into her teenage years, riling up even her father with a stubborn refusal to do what was expected of her.

At school she was bright, and in her last year of primary was encouraged to apply for St Albans. When she eventually took her place there, she recalls being 'good for literally one term', and by then she had had enough. While so many things came naturally to her, she was easily bored and seemed compulsively drawn to disrupting everything.

Both my parents were rebellious at school, but my mother was more hardcore. Dad plotted elaborate pranks and made a point of always looking scruffy, while Mum skipped classes, partied, stole her parents' cars before she could drive and sneaked into pubs long before she turned eighteen. Eventually she was expelled for smoking on the school property during what should have been her final art exam—the last straw in a long list of misdemeanours. She moved in a pack of girls and became inseparable from one in particular, her best friend Philippa. Together they smoked cigarettes and drank gin, upset their teachers and their parents, and played David Bowie loudly on the record player in my mother's bedroom while her parents took her younger sister horse riding.

I don't know what to call it, this rebellious streak. It's so central to my mother's character, and yet so in juxtaposition with the rest of her personality. In some ways she is a hopeless rule abider, always driving under the speed limit, correcting people who give her the wrong change. When I first started working, she insisted I arrive fifteen minutes early every day so as to appear 'keen'. It's not even real rebellion, not now her teenage years have passed—but it's there somehow, the desire to be unpredictable. She'll always want to be the last one awake at a party, just for the sake of it. She never plays music unless she's playing it loudly, until you can't hear yourself singing along. During social occasions where she's supposed to be behaving, she'll raise her eyebrows at you in invitation—a challenge, a prank, the ultimate dare. She attracts people with the same character, giggling as they sneak out of their kids' boring school events for a cigarette.

When she was seventeen, all she wanted was to move to

London. She applied for a job working at Simpsons department store, which she got. Back then, Simpsons was the place to go for the latest fashion—up there with Harrods and Harvey Nichols. The Queen shopped there, all the London socialites shopped there. For my mother it was the height of glamour, and even working on the shop floor was exciting.

*

The same year my mother moved to London, my father was also at the end of his last year of school and deciding what to do next. Growing up, he had wanted to study medicine, never really pausing to question other options. He wasn't a particularly outstanding student—battling through chemistry and physics—but he had good teachers and he scraped by.

In England, you apply to university before you sit your final exams, and then are offered your place depending on your results. So, well before he sat his A Levels, my father applied for medical school. Because his father Richard was Irish, Dad felt drawn to study in Ireland, and so applied for Dublin, Belfast and Dundee. The problem, however, was that those schools were considered academic and, by comparison, the London hospitals of the 70s tended to have a lower academic hurdle but interviewed more rigorously. And so my father, suspecting his grades might not get him to Ireland, applied to St Thomas's Hospital Medical School as well.

When I talk to my family members in various interviews, I am struck by how differently things can be remembered. Dad describes a pervasive feeling of loneliness throughout his childhood, a niggling sense that he was somehow isolated from the people around him. Granny describes a boy who was popular, loved, always laughing. 'He was just . . . happy,' she tells me.

When we come to Dad's interview for St Thomas's, I have to laugh—in my father's version, both his parents are away.

grandfather is house-sitting, a man whom Dad describes as 'stern, not very emotionally connected'. However, he set about trying to help his grandson prepare for the big interview. 'I borrowed his suit,' Dad tells me: 'a three-piece chequered suit, very old school and uncool at the time. He knew nothing at all about medicine and had no idea what they might ask me, but he actually gave me some very sound advice—telling me that if I looked them in the eye, and answered honestly to anything they asked me, I wouldn't go too far wrong. Which is good grandfatherly advice.'

Actually, Granny tells me, they were all at home, and the suit was borrowed from a neighbour who still lives down the road today. I don't know if my father just made up his grandfather's advice, or if perhaps someone else gave it to him, or if it was from another time altogether. I think about this when people ask me what I'm writing. 'Is it a true story?' they want to know. 'Is it made-up names, or will people know it's about you?'

'It's a memoir,' I tell them, a story constructed from memories, selected and sometimes invented, moments imagined by me or someone else. I choose all the pieces that make it in.

Either way, my father admits he doesn't remember much about the actual interview other than talking a lot about rugby, being nervous and feeling embarrassed about his suit. But they obviously liked him, because they gave my father a stupidly low offer—only two Bs and a C needed in his A Levels, and he was in. With the prospect of medical school ahead of him and a new life in London, things were looking up. And then, to his delight, he was finally given the okay to play rugby again, which he'd been barred from because of his injured knees.

He had his first game back playing for the 1st XV. Twenty minutes in he suffered an injury—booted in his left side by a member of the opposing team. He dropped like a tree. At first

31

it appeared as though he was just winded, and indeed it felt to him like he was winded, although the feeling didn't go away. He lay on the pitch for a while, and then was eventually carted off to the sanatorium.

Luckily, the school matron quickly recognised that something was seriously wrong. She called an ambulance, and my father was delivered to the Radcliffe Infirmary. It turned out he had broken his ribs, ruptured his spleen and split his kidney. He underwent an emergency operation, where his spleen was removed and he was administered a six-litre blood transfusion.

The end result was an entire term of school missed and, when it came to his A Levels, he failed the exam he needed to get a C in. His summer travelling plans were put on hold. He stayed at school to repeat physics and, once he had secured his C, he was able to reinstate his place at St Thomas's and arrived in London late at the end of 1978.

My father loved London. Because of his late application, he had missed all the halls of residence, and so ended up sharing a room with a French guy in a shabby flat in Bayswater. He would walk through Hyde Park every day to St Thomas's, often borrowing his roommate's supply of French cheesecloth shirts. St Thomas's was pretty traditional, an actual hospital rather than a university, the students running along the corridors behind their professors, taking notes. But it was also social, his days off spent parked up on the sticky seats of the local pub.

My mother was also happy in London. She had moved into a flat with some of her workmates from Simpsons, and the following years—as she hazily recalls—were a time of constant social activity, clubbing and dancing away long evenings in London's best gay bars. She worked hard, moving up the ranks until eventually she was given a role in the press office, finally able to put her writing skills to good use in press releases and sending selections of clothes to all the big magazines—*Vogue, Tatler, Harpers & Queen*. When I ask her how she felt at the time, she says that mostly she was 'unbelievably excited by everything'. It was social and cool, and she felt right at the centre of it all. Even with the great influx of new friends, she always kept up with Philippa, her best friend from school, who happened to work across the road on Jermyn Street. They would meet for long, wine-fuelled lunches, and would spend their weekends together rotating around their various social groups or taking spontaneous trips away, appreciating the freedom of their own incomes.

Mum still returned home a lot. She was close with her two siblings and, away from fast-paced London, she loved nothing more than spending long afternoons in their local, the White Hart, with all her long-time friends from home. Her brother Andrew worked for their father and played rugby for the local team. On Saturdays—game day—they would all end up at the White Hart, where he, Mum and later their sister Lucy enthusiastically competed in drinking games. It was here where Mum met the Gladstone brothers, a family of four boys who all played for the same rugby team as Andrew. They were an entertaining presence in the White Hart, always together and engaged in banter, the kind of boys everyone knew and wanted to be associated with, because whatever they were doing was bound to be the most fun. It was the first strong sense Mum had that one day she wanted a big family of her own—everyone shouting over each other, the jokes fast and funny.

My father, meanwhile, was growing restless. His first two years at St Thomas's had been preclinical lectures and theory. Pharmacology, biochemistry, anatomy. In his third year he was unleashed on the actual patients; not allowed to do anything, but religiously tailing the doctor on duty as he did his ward round, my father observing and answering questions. The Brixton Riots happened around this time, and

Dad, along with some of the other students, had to help in the emergency department. Usually it was split into a surgical area and a medical area, but during the riots it was separated into injured police on one side and injured protesters on the other. The Special Patrol Group, who were hated at the time for their corrupt and racist behaviour, predominantly made up the police side. Every so often, my father remembers, someone would rise up from either side and make a dash for it, attempting to take a swing at the opposing party.

My father liked working in the emergency department, but at that stage he still resisted giving any consideration whatsoever to his career. While his classmates plotted their next tactical move, my father dreamed of getting away—of dive trips or sailing, of going on an adventure. He kept trying to talk his professors into letting him have a year off, but they refused, firmly informing him that he had to stick it out if he wanted to hold on to his place at St Thomas's.

Eventually my father did finish medical school, graduating in the end of 1983. This was followed by a year of house jobs, in my father's case six months at the fairly prestigious medical professorial unit at St Thomas's, and then on to Exeter. He was in a long-term on-and-off relationship at the time, with a girl he'd met at medical school. She's a part of our family history, even now—the first great love of his life, the two of them driving up and down the country to see each other for weekends and holidays, going away with each other's families, talking about their futures and the trips they planned to go on. My father, now, says that he probably wasn't mature enough for what was happening between them. It was a complicated time for him, and the relationship ended very badly, after ten years together. My siblings and I know all about what happened; my father has often discussed it with us, fretting that we would somehow end up in the same sad situation. When I had my own first heartbreak, during university, I left Wellington briefly to seek refuge at home. To get there involved a flight to Blenheim on a tiny ten-seat plane so horrendously turbulent that I vomited in the space of ten minutes. The relationship had ended only the night before, and having not slept, I spent the flight not only vomiting but also sobbing, a source of alarm for the nine other passengers whom I resolutely ignored. To my relief I was picked up in Blenheim by my worried parents, and driven home to Kaikōura. Later that night, talking with my parents about rejection and heartbreak, my mother and I ended up comforting my tearful father about his final breakup with Charlotte. This ridiculous situation, more than anything else in those first few lonely weeks without my boyfriend, made me laugh.

Talismans

As I write, I stumble across an interview with the author Cheryl Strayed. Her book *Wild* had been passed around my girlfriends when we travelled together through Mexico a few years before, pooling our money and sharing meals and mattresses for weeks on end. I don't know who kept the dog-eared copy when we returned home, but it was one of those books that had us up at night talking, plotting solo adventures and trying to make sense of adulthood—how strong we could be, and how vulnerable. In the interview I listen to, Cheryl talks about teaching her creative writing students to work with prompts. 'What's the best one?' the interviewer asks, and Cheryl says, 'Talismans.'

A talisman, she explains, is an object with accumulated meaning. A thing, or an item, that has some story attached to it, some intrinsic significance. When she asks her students to write about themselves via an object, the writing is usually more meaningful and expansive.

I can see our family's talismans with a swift and unexpected clarity. Dad's pink sailing pants, for example, loose and faded and fraying at the knees. He bought them in the 80s, but they still make regular appearances today—worn after work, surf-casting off the beach or out in the boat, a sign of contentedness, of Dad feeling relaxed.

Once, on a long car trip, someone asked me one of those would-you-rather questions: would you rather be permanently underdressed or overdressed? The question was too easy—I come from a family of underdressers. Growing up, scruffiness was held as a desirable state of being. 'Low key' was a phrase my parents used with positive emphasis, along with 'natural', 'understated', 'humble' and 'no fuss'. To this day, dressing up makes me feel awkward, somehow unlike myself. It's irrational but hardly surprising, given how much of a meal my parents make over being required to wear anything beyond jeans and a T-shirt.

I can always convince Dad of my outfit choices if it's anything vintage or what he would call 'grungy'—faded shirts, long woollen coats, hats of any kind. When he comes to visit me in Wellington, we can spend hours browsing op shops, Dad trying on ancient waistcoats or worn Doc Martens. When I was fifteen, I had my first school semi-formal, and somehow I ended up shopping with Dad. We bought a dark olive green dress with black straps, and, on his suggestion, I wore it with black boots.

His own wardrobe is full of ripped T-shirts and shorts flecked with paint; his go-to outfit for events is a white linen shirt and floral tie. He also has a thing for headscarves—as Mum jokes, 'If he's wearing a headscarf, he's happy.' They're not really headscarves—more like sarongs, long bits of thin fabric that Dad winds round his head when he's any place hot, the material covering his neck and shoulders. In the photos of him young, travelling, he's always wearing them. Now they come out when he's gardening, on the boat, hiking, camping or occasionally at festivals, which my parents sometimes took us to as kids.

When I was sixteen, I went with Dad to a three-day festival in the Mackenzie country. Dad was going for a boys trip with his old mate Dave and a group of guys from Kaikōura; I was going because my mates from Wanaka had invited me down. Dad set up the back of his Land Rover as a kind of refuge for me and my friends, a spot out of the wind and dust and burning sun. We cut up apples with his penknife, ate hummus and crackers, the music echoing down from the stage. Dad bought me a couple of drinks, and then, later, one of the boys I knew passed me a hipflask he'd bought from the two-dollar shop and my eyes watered at the nail-polish taste of straight vodka. In the evenings I disappeared into the festival, Dad sitting around his friends' caravans, the smell of marijuana wafting over while I raised my eyebrow at him, laughing. In the morning we checked out the festival market, sipping hungrily from our water bottles as the sun, even so early, started to burn. Dad bought me a secondhand army bomber jacket, and himself some kind of crocheted vest.

Occasionally I would bump into him on the dancefloor, the two of us grinning at each other, shouting over the music, our faces washed in coloured lights. It reminded me of when I was a little kid at the Kaikōura Roots Festival, dancing for the first time ever with Mum and her friend Susan, their tanned arms moving in time with the music, me clumsily trying to copy.

When I interview my parents now, for this book, I try to imagine them as strangers—try to write without their voices in my head, attempt to hear something new in the stories I've been told a hundred times. We are oddly nervous with each other, my iPhone voice recorder like an intruder in the room, someone who we need to censor ourselves around. In the beginning I suggest we talk over dinner, later regretting it as I listen back to snatches of interview between sounds of chewing and cutlery scraping—an easy way, I discover, to drive myself into a rage. Later, I work out that car journeys are best, preferably long ones when there is nothing else to do but talk, no awkward eye contact to be maintained.

My parents are getting older now—not *old* old, but nearing

sixty, my mother no longer inclined to wear the faded denim miniskirts and singlets that my friends used to comment on when I was in high school ('Your mum looks like a surfer!'). Now she wears shorts and T-shirts, tan lines striping her shoulders from hours spent out in the garden, brown hair pulled back in a ponytail. Across the table, my dad's hair is grey-white, sticking up in all directions, his face tanned and lined. His teeth (crooked) and eyes (green) are the same as they have always been.

No one in our immediate family is what you'd call petite. Compared to some of our English cousins, who are tiny, we joke that we are like a herd of buffalo: muscled legs and arms, the boys now huge at six feet. Even Mum is tall, slim and broad-shouldered. We all have huge heads. An entirely new hat size had to be ordered for my brother Finn when he started primary school.

Dad is constantly scratched or cut from his missions around the house, fixing fences or cutting down trees. 'You're bleeding!' someone will say, and he'll reply, 'Am I?' without much interest, dabbing at his arm or face absentmindedly. Once, he nearly cut his leg in half with a chainsaw while he was chopping wood. 'Bugger,' he mumbled, lying on the grass, pale and sweating. 'I really didn't want to have to go into town today.'

It's not that he's trying to be a hero in these moments, just that he can never be bothered with medical dramas on his days off. Our own injuries are similarly ignored. As a kid I broke my arm falling off my friend's top bunk, and when Dad inspected it he said, 'You'll be right.' He made a makeshift cast for me by strapping a salad spoon to my arm with masking tape, my hand clutching the spoon end. Mum's broken leg, also ignored, not to mention toothaches, earaches and other boring maladies.

At home, our medical kit is full of weird, expired prescription pills and lacks anything remotely helpful like bandaids or Panadol. Dad's Land Rover, too: a treasure trove of once important items or bits of paper, trampled down into the floor, spilling out sometimes when he opens the doors. 'He's a walking fucking cyclone!' Mum will shout, overcome with frustration as she tries to figure out where he's left important bills, his wallet, his keys, his phone, her phone, her keys—anything he's picked up and then absentmindedly put down again.

When I try to think of a talisman that connects the two of us, Dad and me, I think of the wooden carving he brought me back from Nepal; a bull, stocky and dark, a solid little guy on a dyed wooden base. He's been crudely carved, his surface still rough to the touch in places, heavy in my hands. He's sitting on my bedroom windowsill now, faded slightly on one side from the sun. I have a lot of love for him, so uncomplaining, a little banged up but still this strong, staunch animal. I like that Dad found him and thought of me, picked him up and carried him home across oceans, biffing him across the room to me with a grin.

Philippa

When I ask Mum and Dad to talk to me about their lives, it comes out in stories. Nothing sequential—we jump backwards and forwards through countries, ages, boyfriends and girlfriends. When I listen back to our recordings, my first few weeks are spent trying to create some semblance of order, some sense of a timeline. Dad, initially awkward, loosens up as we go along, forgetting about the recorder and spinning off on tangents until I have to remind him to get back on track. We discover that red wine makes a great improvement to our interviews and, slowly, I start to piece it all together, haphazard notes in my journal taking on a shape, something I can visualise.

Dad finished his house jobs in 1984, making him essentially qualified but still very green. He needed work experience, but all he could think about was heading overseas—and so began hatching a plan with Robert, one of his close friends from Radley who had since left school and joined the army. Rob had also been a member of the school dive club, and he and my father had maintained a strong friendship, the two of them meeting up in their holidays to organise diving and sailing trips.

As it happened, a former British Army officer was in the process of setting up a project called Operation Raleigh. The idea was to select a group of young, hardcore adventure-enthusiasts, take them to a remote location and give them a project, ultimately providing them with an inspiring and character-building experience; a way for young people to develop life skills. Operation Raleigh grew over the years, and it is still popular and operational on a global scale today. But back then, in 1984, it was the very first trip, and at that stage still pretty experimental.

Rob, being in the Army, was involved in the programme and had a fairly heavy hand in its creation. He was determined to get Dad on the staff as a doctor, meaning all his travel would be paid for and food provided. The trip was aimed at eighteen- to twenty-four-year-olds, and Rob and my father were only twenty-four themselves. The purpose of the first trip was to go to the Bahamas and explore the 'blue holes', an extensive cave system that ran underneath the reef. There were some genuinely knowledgeable cave divers on the trip who would be videoing and researching, so the trip had a quasi-legitimate exploratory purpose. My father was also a qualified dive instructor at that point, adding to Rob's case for securing him a job.

In hindsight, my father's enthusiasm for the trip was pretty naive. Despite his years of study, he was still very inexperienced and would have struggled if someone had a serious illness or injury. But from his point of view it was the dream job—travel paid, three months on a deserted island in the Bahamas, diving all day, young people. He didn't dwell so much on what could go wrong, and when Rob called to tell him the job was his, he simply sold his car, put his possessions in storage and left for the Bahamas.

There were a few serious divers, about thirty 'venturers'—the young people who had applied and been selected to come along—and then the staff, including Rob and Dad. They arrived on an army supply boat, and were unceremoniously dumped on the beach with everything it was predicted they might need—tents, food, compressors, dive gear. Basically, they were left to get on with it.

Thankfully, there were no major injuries on that trip, no serious drama. Dad had brought with him a load of carefully selected army medical supplies, although as it turned out he had missed a few essentials. Expecting tropical infections, he was quickly alarmed to discover that he hadn't stocked up things like contraception—much to the bemoaning of the fellow venturers. Still, despite the occasional worry it was easily the most fun he had ever had, days spent exploring the network of underwater caves, fishing and lying on the beach under the sun.

When his three months in the Bahamas were up, he immediately wanted to join up with the next trip, which was scheduled to take place in Honduras. He made plans to travel with a guy from the first trip called Mike O'Byrne, and the two of them set off together, catching a ride on an army supply boat as far as the Yucatán Peninsula in Mexico.

Mike was an interesting character, wild and gutsy. Ex special forces, he until recently had been undercover in Belfast, being hunted by the IRA. In Ireland he'd been the youngest serving officer of the time, and was on the IRA's most wanted list. Things had turned sour when some of his platoon had been killed in a bomb attack. Mike had managed to capture some of the men responsible, but then a grief-stricken member of his platoon had beaten one of them up in holding, and killed him. Mike had been court martialed, held responsible because he was in charge. Out of a job, he'd volunteered for the Bahamas trip, and he and my father had hit it off.

When they reached the Yucatán Peninsula, they made the pretty rash decision to travel the rest of the way on foot. My father remembers this trip as a strange and unsettling one, a month of slow but gruelling travel—Mexico through to

Guatemala, and then eventually into Honduras. Because of Mike's lingering paranoia from his days in Ireland, and to avoid the heat of the day, they walked mostly at night, sleeping hidden during the day in ditches along the roadside. My father was impressed with Mike's survival skills and was able to enjoy the trip despite its unsettling structure. But, as he would soon discover, this sense of unease was only preparation for what was to come—when the two of them arrived at their destination, they found no great sense of relief.

While their time in the Bahamas had been sunny and simple, Honduras proved a different beast. For a start, the project was a lot less structured—they were supposed to be doing archaeological work, but at the last minute the government announced that the work wasn't allowed, and so activities were hastily reorganised.

'The vibe was just different,' my father tells me, 'humid and jungly. There was an edge to it. There was a lot of tension between the locals—those of Spanish descent and then the Carib ex-slave population on the mangrove swamp side of the island. The whole thing had more of an atmosphere, and we had a slightly more rowdy group. It just got loose, I guess, it was a bit out of control. Nothing terrible happened, but there was sort of this vague feeling of tension. At one point a group of us shaved our hair into Mohicans—I don't know why, just because we could. It felt like anything could happen.'

Dad mostly spent his evenings with Mike, the two of them canoeing over to a local bar that hung out over the swampy water, an open-sided low-lit shack complete with a couple of pool tables and a jukebox. They hummed along to 'Sultans of Swing', slapping mosquitoes away from their eyes and drinking warm spirits from dirty glasses.

During the day my father would be kept busy by visiting locals, who would often seek him out wanting treatment. This caused him a fair amount of anxiety; not only did he lack the right equipment, but he didn't have a lot of experience. People would arrive to the army camp with various injuries or illnesses, usually just needing antibiotics or wounds to be dressed, but occasionally they would ask my father to make house visits. Luckily there was another medic on this trip, a nurse whom my father had befriended and who would travel with him into the villages surrounding their camp. Often the patients would be young children or babies, usually with infections or tropical sores. With language barriers and only basic medical supplies, my father worried about these trips, knowing that at some point he would arrive to a scene that was beyond him.

One humid morning, he woke to find a local woman outside his tent who explained in broken English that he was needed at her village. She was there on behalf of a teenage girl who had been in labour for two days and was in bad shape. My father and the nurse agreed to go, setting off with some trepidation through the mangrove swamp by boat, an eerie and unsettling journey, quiet apart from the sound of their oars cupping the water. The day before, two men had arrived to camp after some kind of altercation, both badly beaten, dried blood and bruises, a nose smashed in. My father trailed his hand in the water as they crept along, violence humming beyond the swamp and through the trees.

When they arrived at the little shack, there was a woman inside lying on a mat, bleeding heavily and drifting in and out of consciousness. It was muggy, and she was slick with sweat. She had been in labour for a long time and, although some of the local midwives were there, nobody seemed sure what to do or how to help, which only added to my father's general sense of alarm. Excitement in the small group rose at his arrival— the white doctor who would save the day. In reality my father was twenty-four years old, had no idea about obstetrics and was feeling scarily ill-prepared.

All he could think to do was sit down in front of her and try and to see what was going on. He was relieved that the woman was nearly unconscious, as he didn't have any painkillers on hand and had no choice but to be forceful. Although he had gloves on, my father remembers the sickening moment he looked down at his collection of hippy string bracelets around his wrist, now covered in blood—hardly sanitary. He felt overwhelmed and out of his depth, with no plan other than to try and haul the baby out with his hands.

The only grip he could get was on the baby's head, and he was seriously concerned that by pulling with such force he was bound to rip its head off. He pulled anyway, hoping that, even if the baby died, at least there would be hope for saving its mother. But to his astonishment, after ten or so minutes of pulling, the baby spilled into his arms.

'I completely expected it to be dead, or that I'd somehow injured it. The whole process had, on my part, been pretty forceful and awful. But then—to my absolute amazement— the baby just started crying, and began doing all the normal things babies are meant to do when they've just been born. And, thank god, the mother didn't bleed to death from a postpartum haemorrhage, which in hindsight is absolutely remarkable. So they all lived to tell the tale. But the whole thing was pretty traumatic. There's a photo of me later, holding the baby—I went back to visit it. And they both really did survive. And they called the baby Christopher.'

*

Back in England, my mother had taken a job for Welsh fashion designers David and Elizabeth Emanuel. When she first arrived to their press office they were in the process of creating Princess Diana's wedding dress, and initially her days were spent managing the media storm that swirled through London and, as my mother sincerely believed, the whole world. *I'm working for the Emanuels*, she would say to herself, disbelieving.

She worked with the Emanuels for a year before getting a more senior role at the iconic Lloyd's of London, working in their PR office right in the centre of town. She's taken me back to that old building—winding through cobbled streets tracing her daily commute, heels clipping on stone. It's a bookstore now, still with its pillared entrance and grand facade. We walked around inside, weaving through throngs of shoppers. She shrugged her shoulders at the garish colours of the children's section, plastic pens and stuffed animals. 'Another world, I guess,' she said, and we moved on.

She was home one weekend when she met Ian. He was halfway through a pint in the White Hart, catching up with old friends when my mother arrived, breathless and laughing. He was stationed in Cape Town working for an oil drilling company, back for a month on a home visit. He was good-looking and funny, and my mother liked the way time moved when they were together—rushing past, seamless, never stopping to assert itself.

Ian was the kind of person who knew what he wanted, that was clear. They went out to nice restaurants, charmed each other's families over bottles of wine. They were engaged within the year, my mother's parents beaming at her when she shared the news, Ian holding on tightly to her hand.

He invited her to come and live with him in Cape Town while he worked out the remainder of his contract. An overseas adventure appealed to my mother, South Africa with its rocky landscape and looser rules. Cape Town took her breath away, full of interesting people, rugged edges and boozy nights out. Ian had friends everywhere, and Mum's life seemed to be expanding—always a new place to spend her afternoons and evenings, a new rotation of friends dropping by to visit, new shift dresses cinched in at the waist.

But the glow was starting to fade. Ian was becoming more

and more possessive, alarming her on a number of occasions with his quick rage, pulling her up for things she hadn't even noticed. 'What are you talking about?' she would ask over and over, while he railed at her for looking at other men, talking to people he didn't like, not sitting beside him at dinner.

One night they met up with some of my mother's friends from London, a dinner spent laughing and sharing stories, their limbs golden from days spent in the sun. When they returned home later that evening, Ian exploded, screaming at my mother for passing an unwanted slice of pizza down the table to her old friend Dan. Ian's fury at this gesture—over the preference he believed her to have shown—was so swift and so alarming that my mother spent the next few nights tiptoeing around their home, which suddenly felt cold and very far from home.

She called Philippa, who was still working in London. 'Come home,' Philippa told her, 'and then tell him. But come home first.'

She told him she needed to return to England to plan their wedding. This wasn't unreasonable; the invites had already been sent. They kissed goodbye before she left, my mother smiling, her suitcase heavy in her hand. When she got home she rang him up and called the whole thing off. Philippa stood beside her while they talked. 'You're joking,' Ian had said to her, quietly and then louder. But she wasn't joking. She hung up the phone and Philippa clapped for her, both women shivering with what could have been.

Nearly a year later, my mother found herself repeating Ian's words—a different phone call, Cape Town far behind her. The phone rang in the morning, her friend Mark on the other end of the line. 'It's Philippa,' he said. 'I'm so sorry, Esther. I'm so sorry.' Philippa had been about to get married; Mark was going to be best man at the wedding. 'You're joking,' my mother said, once and then three times. 'It's not funny,' she whispered into the silence on the end of the phone. Philippa had spent the night in with her fiancé. They'd had dinner and were watching TV on the couch. She suffered a brain aneurysm, a swift and sudden end to her short life.

When I ask her about it, my mother can't really remember the exact feeling—the world shifting, her best friend in a coffin. Death felt strange and suffocating, so significant and somehow so far away. Philippa's wedding was six weeks away, and so all her favourite songs and prayers and flowers had already been discussed. In its own strange way the wedding went ahead, weeks early and missing the beautiful bride, her laughter and her warm body.

'I don't know what drew us together so much,' my mother tells me. 'There was just something about her. We laughed so much. We always just wanted to be around each other.'

They had the funeral and then a wake at her parents' house, where my mother had spent nights laughing with Philippa's mum and dad, sneaking drinks from their liquor cabinet. After she died so many of my mother's friendships dissipated. Philippa had seemed to connect them all, and without her London felt bigger: its pulse slow, cold streets, dark afternoons.

*

While my mother navigated life without Philippa, my father returned to England for work. He had applied for a vocational GP training scheme run over three years, highly competitive to get into. At the time, Exeter Medical School—which ran the training scheme—was considered to be at the forefront of GP training: very progressive, process-focused, emphasis placed on interactions with patients and communication. My father was accepted and, as part of his training, began working as junior GP in a local medical practice. Alongside the day-to-day work there was a focus on self-analysis, which my father equal parts hated and appreciated, recalling having to watch terrible videos of himself in consultation. The practice where he worked was in a little town called Tiverton, just outside the city. Tiverton sparked in my father a love for rural practice, although it offered a somewhat romantic view—friendships with locals, trout fishing in the evenings, a broad scope of work.

With the Honduras delivery still ringing in his head, he decided to take a year-long obstetric job. During his vocational training he had done a three-month gynaecological course, but he still felt haunted by the sight of that young mother, limp and sweating on the floor of her hut. He knew that if he wanted to travel the world as a doctor—which he did—he needed to learn about delivering babies. Still, however necessary it may have felt, my father reflects on that year as a brutal one. Being the doctor, he generally wasn't required to attend deliveries that were going well; instead he was called in when something was amiss or going badly. If someone had a tear, or a bleed, or the baby was stuck or needed resuscitation, that's when my father was requested.

Sitting around the table with two beers and my iPhone recording, Dad tells me that, even though he knows it's irrational, he is terrified at the thought of me having a baby. 'I don't know,' he says, 'I just find it really unnerving. At the start of a birth, everyone's fine—mother and baby, both fine. There is also an absolute expectation that everything's going to stay that way too, that everyone will be okay, and even that it will be a transforming, beautiful experience. Which is great, but you have everything to lose. I mean, it can go really well, obviously. I always say to myself: "Women have done this for millennia! It's fine, it's a natural process!" But I suppose, in contrast, say you're dealing with a car accident—well, the damage has already been done. You're not likely to make anything worse; generally you can only make things better.

Obstetrics has a totally different framework to other aspects of medicine, because you're starting with someone who's well and potentially it can all go wrong. Actually, that's not always true, because now we do a lot of preventative medicine. We have a big responsibility to maintain wellness. But that can be stressful in a similar way, because if you miss someone's high blood pressure, or, say someone has a heart attack and you realise you've forgotten to ask them about their family history, then it turns out their dad's had a heart attack . . . If you'd known, you obviously would have treated them more aggressively. There are a lot of potential pitfalls. I suppose I mean that, in medicine, you're only as good as your next mistake. And it's hard to be perfect.'

Later, when Dad gets called out and heads into town to whatever medical drama is happening, I mention these feelings of his to Mum. 'Burns, too,' she adds. 'He hates burns.' I don't know what particular episode sparked a dislike for burns, but it seems like once he left medical school, the fears started creeping in. Maybe it's because as he grew older his work became higher stakes, the consequences more real. I feel a little sorry for this imagined, boyish father of mine, rushing between births during his year of obstetrics, always trying to do right by everyone and taking so many knocks. But, as it happened, that year would soon be far behind him. Although he didn't know it right then, Dad's life was about to take a turn for the better. That was the year he got a call from John Watson.

Windfall

Dad has loved boats for as long as I can remember. When we were kids, our parents would drive us north or south for camping holidays, the seven of us packed into the Land Rover, my brothers physically fighting over the top of me in the middle, each of us taking turns to vomit as we wound over the hills. If ever we passed a harbour, or if our destination was close to a harbour, we would somehow end up there. Dad was never explicit about wanting to see the boats; he never asked us if we wanted to come. But our walks would wind up at the water, and then we would find ourselves trailing along behind him, yachts bobbing up and down on either side of us.

Sometimes I would sit along the edges of the dock, my feet dangling, watching Dad weave along the rows of boats, pointing out the features whose names I could never remember. Hulls and sails, everything gleaming white and heavy. It was less romantic the closer you got, when all the wires and bolts and rust came into focus. I liked the boats better from afar, sitting on the water like a flock of birds.

Dad often spent evenings at home looking up boats on the internet. First on dial-up and then, in the age of broadband, Trade Me. He spent hours poring over them, the same way he would on the docks. Mum and I often talked about his obsession with sailing. She told me that, every so often, she and Dad would each write down the top five things they wanted from life, as a way of seeing if they were on the right track. 'My own boat,' Dad's always said. He meant a yacht, a sailing boat. He likes the ones that are 'rustic', as he calls them—wooden, beautiful, the right size or shape to fit all of us at a push. He would mumble all this to himself as he scrolled, every so often demanding our opinion as he pondered which one he would get if he could. Looking at yachts always seemed to put him in a good mood, although for years I couldn't help but feel guilty whenever I thought about it. What did it mean to long to be at sea, but never get there? It seemed such a simple thing. The ocean, a fishing rod, taut sails and the smell of salt, a slightly airless cabin. The photographs on our walls started to feel like some kind of torture: Dad, young, hanging off the mast and grinning. Dad up on deck, absorbed in some kind of knot-tying, barefoot and shirtless, happy.

*

John Watson's yacht was called *Windfall*. John was an old friend of my father's parents—he'd grown up in Hong Kong, but as a young man had purchased a house just down the road from my grandparents in Surrey. A keen sailor himself, John enjoyed my father's company and natural ability on the water. The two of them had already done a few sailing trips together during Dad's holidays throughout school and university, including the South China Sea Race from Hong Kong to the Philippines. My father looked up to John, admiring his passion for life and sense of adventure. John was—and is—a kind and warm person, as well as being single-minded, steely and hard-working—traits that make him a rather formidable businessman.

In 1988 he had just sold his stockbroking business in Hong Kong and had purchased a sailboat. He was adamant about joining the prestigious Royal Hong Kong Yacht Club, which was rather frosty towards newcomers. To be welcomed into the club, you either had to be put forward by existing members (and go through a rigorous application process) or you could automatically gain membership by circumnavigating—sailing around the world. In typical headstrong fashion, John had decided the latter was the most appealing of these two options. He began preparing for the epic journey, putting together a crew and gathering everything he would need for eighteen months at sea. By the time he called my father, he had already completed the first leg of the trip up the Indian Ocean and through the Red Sea to the Mediterranean.

Somewhere in the Red Sea, one of John's crewmembers had been hit by the boom and suffered a nasty cut, requiring him to be sent home to England. Reflecting on the issue, John had decided that he needed a doctor onboard. He called up my father and asked him if he had any plans for the next year. That was that and, as soon as his obstetric job ended, my father flew to Palma, met up with John and boarded the boat as crew.

They sailed from Palma to Gibraltar and then to the Canary Islands, where they met up with a group of boats sailing across the Atlantic in a race called the ARC. When my father was on night watch, he'd play music to keep himself awake. John had a pretty limited selection on board, but Dad recognised Nana Mouskouri—a Greek singer his mother used to listen to, back at the Old House in Pirbright. He played 'Je chante avec toi Liberté' over and over, loud enough that it became just that song, him and the ocean. Years later, he chose this song for the first dance at his wedding.

'There is something about the sea,' he tells me. 'Up on deck, middle of the night, powering across—playing that song became just the most evocative thing. I was so free, so out-there.' At night, the ocean would sometimes glow in a long flare of bioluminescent phytoplankton, the microscopic organisms that float in the upper sunlit layers of the ocean. In concentrated numbers, they would light up the surface, phosphorescent. Clustered with stars and phytoplankton, the black night sky and the ocean felt inseparable, as though Dad was travelling through space, the only human thing in the vast, rolling darkness.

He describes to me the feeling of total self-sufficiency, so far from land and home. 'You have to live off your wits, in a way,' he says. And it's true—if something went wrong, it was just him and the unforgiving ocean. 'But that's why the sea is particularly empowering, because it's so frightening. We were so far from anywhere . . . you just head out there and then keep on heading. You're by yourself. You know, if I went for a pee in the middle of the night and fell of the back, I'd be dead.'

When the boat eventually sailed into the Caribbean, my father talked John into letting him have three weeks off in Antigua, promising to catch up with the boat in Tortola after John had spent some time with his family and my father had had a chance to do some sightseeing.

Antigua was buzzing with people, some arriving from long months and sea, some having spent months on the island trying to find work. It was hot and beachy and a relief for Dad to be able to park up at the local bar and relax, to find his feet on solid ground again. It was here, in the bar, that my father met a woman called Miranda, whose parents had just returned to England but who had left her alone for a week with their yacht. She liked Dad, and asked if he would come and help her sail the boat the following day. He arrived to find Miranda and a small group of her friends: an English guy called Andrew, Andrew's friend Ian Franklin, and an Australian guy called Simon whom everybody referred to as Mick Dundee. Although my father's hopes of seducing Miranda were quickly quashed, the five of them spent the week laughing their way around the Caribbean on Miranda's boat, Dad convinced this was surely the best thing that ever happened to him. Dad formed an instant bond with Andrew, who was wild and charming and hilarious, seemingly up for anything. The boat Andrew had been working on had come into some kind of financial disaster, and so Andrew was parked up in Antigua hoping to find more work. The two of them began spending their evenings together in the bar, and my father quickly came to love Andrew for his genuine kindness and outrageous sense of fun. Late one night in the bar, Andrew confessed his troubles to my father: he was down to his last $75 and had no idea what he would do next. My father was due to fly to Tortola the next day to meet up with John and, fuelled by alcohol, he assured Andrew that John would have work for him. The next day, hungover but with no other options, Andrew spent his last dollars on a ticket to Tortola, and flew out with Dad.

Arriving in Tortola, my father started feeling nervous. In reality he had no idea how John would feel about his plan to recruit Andrew, whom he now felt responsible for. My father instructed Andrew to wait for him in the bar next to the marina, and went ahead to find John. John was initially pleased to see Dad, but then quick to snap at him that they certainly didn't need any more crew, and couldn't understand why my father was suggesting it. Dad then had to confess to John that Andrew was waiting in the bar nearby, and had no more money because my father had promised him a job. John was furious and shouted at Dad that he was an idiot, promising to find Andrew himself and tell him to hightail it back to Antigua.

John stormed off down the jetty towards the bar, telling my father to wait in the boat. Dad recounts pacing in agony, feeling guilty for letting down Andrew and suggesting the whole plan in the first place. Not sure what to do, he waited for them both to return, but nothing happened—neither turned up. He waited for hours before eventually deciding he would head for the bar himself and see what happened. As he began to walk down the jetty he heard singing, and looked up to see John and Andrew arm in arm and completely pissed, staggering down towards the boat together. Andrew was installed that night.

*

By the time my father returned to England, he and Andrew had become close friends. Over many long days and nights at sea they had shared their lives with each other, discussing their families, relationships, their plans and hopes for the future. Andrew was planning to continue on *Windfall* after my father left, but promised they would catch up as soon as he was back on English soil. 'After all,' he said out of nowhere as they hugged goodbye, 'you need to meet my sister, because you're going to marry her.' My father laughed and protested at this, but Andrew was serious. 'I'm sorry,' he said, 'I know it sounds strange. But she's the one for you.' My father was taken aback by Andrew's insistence, and he brushed the comment aside.

When Andrew did return home, nearly a year later, he organised a welcome-back weekend in Salcombe, the seaside village where he'd spent his summers growing up. He told my mother that Chris was coming—the guy he'd spent all that time sailing with, the guy he'd told her so much about. It was a blatant set-up, Mum's friends teasing her days before Dad was due to arrive, which he eventually did, walking into the Ferry Inn with faded pink shorts and a worn T-shirt. Andrew shouted a welcome from across the room, and the two of them embraced, each laughing at how strange the other looked in this familiar English setting.

Later, at dinner, my parents sat beside one another, and by the time everyone was leaving, they had decided they wanted to stay. 'We might just have one more drink,' my mother said sheepishly, while her friends raised their eyebrows at her, laughing.

The following months for my parents were spent driving between London and Exeter, nervously at first and then with increasing confidence. In a way they were a strange fit, my mother still very much a London girl, frightening my father with her tailored suits and shiny shoes while he went tanned and barefoot.

They went to visit Manor Farm, meeting Grandma Anne over a long lunch in her heady flower garden. Mum recalls that while Dad was talking, he started unconsciously grinding his knife down into the beautiful wood of her mother's outdoor table, while Anne looked on in barely disguised horror. But still he won her over, another piece of the puzzle falling into place and confirming my parents' belief that Andrew had predicted their marriage because it was something bigger than them, something inevitable. Over weekends and nights out, my parents watched on as old friends they had known for years met and laughed and loved each other. My mother finally had her own version of the Gladstone brothers: the four Henry boys, a whirlwind group she could fall into as though she had always been there.

One weekend, less than a year after the Salcombe dinner that had thrown them together, they rented a little cottage in Sark, an island in the southwestern English Channel, off the coast of France. My father was a locum at the local hospital, and my mother came out to meet him with Andrew, Dad's brother Harry and his wife Louise. That afternoon Dad looked over at Mum, about to change for dinner, and asked her if she wanted to get married. He didn't have a ring, but she said yes, and they shouted the news downstairs to the others. Andrew sprinted down to the local pub and bought every bottle of champagne they had.

I've heard the stories from their wedding day, turned the heavy pages of the photo albums. Fred, who ran the White Hart pub, organised two shire horses and borrowed a carriage from the local brewery with 'COURAGE' spelled out across the back of it. There's a photo of my mother sitting in the carriage, just married, flowers in her hair. Grandma Anne had made the flower crown, and all day—too heavy—it slipped into my mother's eyes. In the photos, she looks too happy to care.

Africa

It's getting colder in Wellington, now the middle of the year. Everything is beginning to weigh down on me—my writing, the wind, the rain which feels so endless, soaking the worn-down canvas of my shoes. Every year around this time I realise that I don't own any practical clothes. I dredge up a raincoat from a dusty box under the stairs. I need new thermals. All my money is tied up in my flat account, so I can go on living in Wellington while I write. Rent is covered—it's everything else that feels stressful. The kids whom I nanny cry that they are freezing when we walk home from school, their small, cold hands intertwined with mine. My bedroom window doesn't close properly and the rain pours through the gaps, drenching a stack of books and leaving a puddle on the carpet. I go out to a party. 'How are you?' everyone asks, and all I can think about is how much I want the rain to stop.

I decide to move in with a friend—if we share a room, we can halve our rent. We plot how this will work over beers at Laundry bar. It's two in the morning and we are sure it's the best idea we've ever had. It actually is a great idea—even when we've danced off the alcohol, purchased twin beds, found replacements for our old flats, packed our things and are living in Thorndon, it still feels right. I like sharing a room. Maybe it's because so much of the time I would otherwise be alone, writing, but there is something nice about it, having someone to unravel the day with, minus romantic complications or expectations. For whatever reason we don't annoy each other, spreadeagled on our beds every evening, laughing about how miserable winter is. We're sure we're meant to be more mature, more adult than all this, but somehow that only makes it seem funnier. Thank god you're here, we say to each other over and over again—imagine if we had do all this on our own!

It's kind of strange living in Thorndon. It's never been my side of town—the business side, the law school and the flash department stores, the most expensive New World in existence. I miss Mt Cook and Newtown, the haphazardness, the ramen shop, the weatherboard houses in their varying states of decline. Lambton Quay feels like a totally different city, everyone walking with so much purpose. I cross through the gardens of parliament to get to work, wondering, like everyone else, who will be elected into government this year. Once I get caught in a legalise-weed protest, winding its way through the grass in a relaxed fashion. I cut down to the waterfront, every time amazed this corporate action takes place so close to the sea.

Friends and family have started gifting me things that might be helpful for my writing. Initially it feels stressful, an unwanted reminder that people know what I'm doing, that they are expecting me to come up with something. But soon I am poring over it all, grateful and emotional. Granny posts me all the emails she has saved, sent by my parents from various exotic locations as they travelled. Printed out, the emails are impossible to decipher in places where the ink has obviously run low. Some of them are pages long and stapled together, and the whole lot have been numbered by hand, a way to keep track of what was sent when. The catalogue goes back so far—if my parents ever needed proof they were loved, this would be it. Family friends send emails, photos, stories of long-forgotten escapades dragged from the depths of memory and kindly written down for me. Mum sends me a bunch of stuff from home, amongst it all a small black diary, its pages filled with her familiar handwriting. I am shocked, because I've never seen it before: the journal she kept in Africa.

I already know a bit about their time in Africa. As well as the diary now, I have two of the three books they took with them: *Stay Alive in the Desert* by K.E.M. Melville and *Sahara Handbook* by Simon and Jan Glen. Only *Africa Overland* is missing, and my parents can't remember the actual name of its author and his travelling companions—they only ever referred to them as 'Mick and the Bandits'. 'How much fuel do we need to get through Bangui?' my parents would ask, flipping through the pages of their dog-eared books. 'What do Mick and the Bandits have to say?' This collection of authors were more than just helpful guides—they were fellow comrades, concrete proof that my parents' insane plan was actually possible. Mum and Dad clung to those books, finding comfort in their words, their advice, their helpful diagrams and long, detailed checklists.

Africa was their honeymoon—a year-long drive from bottom to top. The names sat strangely in their mouths: Algeria, Sahara, Niger. Impossible expanses of jungle and sand, oppressive heat and violence. It was a dangerous trip, ribboned through with the bright glow of *just married*. It wasn't exactly my mother's idea of a honeymoon, but it also seemed a natural follow-up to their whirlwind romance and wedding. It was out of the ordinary, and they approached it like they did their entire relationship: in one mad, bursting tumble forwards.

My grandfather Richard had lent my parents some money, which they would pay back the following year on their return home, when everyone hoped the two of them would finally settle down. With their own savings, and following the guidebooks,

Mum and Dad began the lengthy process of preparing the vehicle for its journey. As well as installing a safe under the seat, Dad welded on an extra pipe underneath the car, where they could hide the American dollars they were essentially smuggling in to exchange on the black market. They added an extra fuel tank to go alongside the ten army-green jerry cans that Fred and Kim, who ran the White Hart, had given them as a wedding present. They packed in endless Marks and Spencer tins of Chunky Chicken, freeze-dried potatoes and bacon. Dad fitted out metal grilles over the windows to prevent people smashing them in. Spare car parts were loaded in, and a tent was attached to the roof racks. There was an expensive water filter and more jerry cans for water, a medical kit, a can opener, a solar shower—absolutely everything and anything the books instructed went into the car, which my parents had parked up at Pirbright for the weeks before their departure.

When it was time to leave they drove from Dover, catching the ferry that would take them to France, where they could then drive through Spain and eventually into Morocco. Their families came to wave a brutal goodbye—with handwritten letters the only regular means of communication, no one knew how long it would be until they heard each other's voices again. My mother and father waved from the outdoor deck until their parents and brothers disappeared into the ocean, the wake from the ferry streaming out behind them like a final outstretched arm.

Morocco was their first African border-crossing, one of many on their long and somewhat daunting list. My parents dreaded those days, changing out of their shorts and into more appropriate long, loose skirts and pants, relying on their high-school French to convince the customs officers to let them through. The fact they shared the same birthday came up without fail, causing suspicion and incredulity.

'Your wife must have been so cheap!' more than one officer observed, when they eventually decided my parents weren't lying. 'She's not even one day younger than you!'

'Very, very cheap,' my father agreed solemnly, my mother rolling her eyes.

Each day was a series of problems to solve: managing the car, eating, plotting where to sleep. There was a lot of driving, their few CDs on repeat, air rushing through the open windows and coating them in dust and sand. They tried to avoid cities and towns, choosing instead to camp a little way off the roadside, hidden enough to set up their chairs and makeshift kitchen, eating hot food off their gas cooker. Sometimes they would think they were alone only to wake and find themselves surrounded by a ring of curious faces, silent observers watching to see what they might do next. The roof-tent flipped out so that the rest of the roof could be used as a place to sit, and this is what my parents did each day, unfolding their chairs on the roof of the car, sitting and talking and playing music.

There is a photo of my mother sitting in the Sahara looking out across the dunes, her face turned terracotta in the early evening light. When I ask my dad how it felt to be there, alone in such a barren landscape, he said it felt exhilarating. He looks back on his time in Africa as a happy one—a feeling that carries a lot of weight for someone like him, who finds happiness so evasive, slipping like water through his hands.

They had a map, Dad navigating the way through the desert using mountains as landmarks. They listened to Labi Siffre and Frank Sinatra, rolling through the sand with 'New York, New York' swelling into the horizon. They passed through Morocco and into Algeria, where they crossed the Sahara. They travelled into Niger and then Benin, a straight track across the centre of Africa.

After Benin they reached Nigeria, where they were hoping

to pick up precious letters from their family at the post shop in Lagos. They had been told to avoid getting caught in busy towns at sundown, but they misjudged the time it would take them to reach the city centre. After the rolling expanse of empty desert, Lagos felt ominous and overwhelming, packed with people, and as my parents made to leave a crowd began to gather around the car. Boxed in and discussing their options, my parents decided to try and call the British Embassy from the payphone at the post shop—a decision which started to feel more and more justified as hands began pushing the car from side to side. Dad left Mum with the doors locked and pushed through the crowd, hands pulling at his clothes.

'Have you lost your passports?' the Scottish voice on the phone asked. 'No,' Dad said, 'but we're about to.'

'Sit tight,' the voice said. 'Lock the doors and don't get out.'

It was less than five minutes before they heard a blaring horn coming from a jeep that parted the crowd. A head appeared through the window, shouting, 'Follow me!' Next thing they knew, my parents were sitting by the pool of the British Embassy in Lagos, drinking very strong gin and tonics poured by the enthusiastic Scotsman who had rescued them. As it turned out, it was Burns Night—the one night a year Scottish people celebrate their much-loved poet Robbie Burns. Dad knew about Burns Night from his old teacher John Wiley, and predicted it would be only a short amount of time until the whisky appeared, which it did, held triumphantly.

After several days nursing their hangovers at the British Embassy in Lagos, my parents decided it was time to get back on the road. They travelled from Nigeria into Cameroon, then into the Central African Republic. They spent Christmas Eve waiting in line at a payphone for four hours to call home, only to find that there were no international phonelines. Christmas was a miserable occasion—it had been months since they'd talked to any of their family members, and they knew that by now everyone would be seriously worried about them. 'The worst Christmas,' Mum writes, an unusually short and defeated entry in her black diary, 'missing home.'

After Christmas came Zaire, an enormous country with only one, impossible road, pot-holed and muddy, a slow and messy traverse from east to west. Some sections of road were torn with what seemed like trenches, turning what should have been minutes of driving into hours and days. A passing tourist bus, which had stopped to tow my parents through a muddy section of road, suggested they travel by river. The river in question was the Congo, that brooding body of water weaving its way west through Zaire. Big barges travelled up and down it from port to port for trading, and they were known to pick up vehicles and carry them further upstream.

After some investigation, my parents arranged for such a pick up. The barge in question was a large, flat-bottomed vessel with a tin roof, fifty metres long and loaded underneath with vast containers full of grain. Their Land Rover had by then become their beloved home, and they watched in alarm as it was picked up by crane and swung precariously out over the river, dropped onto the empty deck of the barge. My parents were thrilled when they finally boarded—they set up their chairs and tables, the boat moving them quickly through the rainforest, across the heart of Africa. The barge was gloriously empty, and they plotted beers and sunbathing, congratulating each other on their stroke of luck.

After about a mile, the barge stopped again at the side of the river. It was met by a swarm of people who poured on deck, jostling shoulder to shoulder, weighed down with chickens and baskets and cloth and various food items. My parents hurriedly grabbed their chairs and relocated up to the roof of their car, where they watched the deck fill to capacity, until people were piling over the bonnet of the car and setting up shop on top of it.

My parents soon adjusted to the sunny, rolling chaos of the barge, watching in excitement as little trading canoes loaded with food or fabric would launch at great speed from shore, pitching out towards the boat and paddling furiously to reach it. As the other passengers whooped and shouted, these little canoes would try and latch on, their efforts inciting either roars of approval or jeers of shame. The water was teeming with life, and as the party moved down the river the distinct slither of crocodiles could be heard, slipping from the muddy banks and cruising into the water.

It seemed that African life in its entirety was happening on that barge. Cooking, trading, socialising—the hum of busy lives playing out to the backdrop of dense rainforest, a world barely revealed as they slipped along its dark edges. To go to the bathroom required pushing your way through the crowds and dangling over the back rail. Because everybody cooked with palm oil, the rail quickly became slippery, making the whole experience less and less appealing—or even possible— as the days went by. Mum resorted to going in a bucket on the roof, which Dad would then uncomplainingly carry aloft through the throng of people, to tip it over the barge's edge into the river below.

Next to the car one night, a young woman was braiding another woman's hair into tiny spikes that stood up all over her head. Dad asked to have his braided the same way, and the girls obliged, shrieking with laughter afterwards as they told him it was a hairstyle young women used to advertise their single status.

Mum and Dad continued playing their CDs loudly from the car stereo, a move that made them popular among other passengers and each night would draw a crowd of people pushing through to dance along in crushingly close quarters. On New Year's Eve three young guys from Tasmania joined the boat, waving to my parents enthusiastically from across the deck. Eventually they clambered up onto the roof of the car, and the five of them stayed up there all evening, eating crocodile steaks and drinking beers, dancing to Frank Sinatra until Dad thought the roof of the car was going to cave in. At midnight, Dad set off some emergency flares that he had brought for their time in the desert and thankfully hadn't had to use. The flares squealed into the air, exploding above their heads in a cascade of red, a brand new year rolling out ahead of them.

*

Weeks later they were back on the road, this time with another couple from England whom they had joined up with, also in a Land Rover and completing a similar journey. They had picked up some Swiss hitchhikers from the last village, who were now sitting on the roof of my parent's car as it rolled along. The map they carried with them said they were beside a national park, and the group had decided it could be an interesting place to visit and spend the night.

They drove off the main road and made for the park, driving for hours up a tiny switchback track into the mountains. They had no idea what they were looking for, but at the top the park was empty and derelict; what had once been a campground was abandoned and dilapidated. Disappointed but exhausted, the group decided to stay for the night. Just as they were settling in, a soldier appeared from the bush and asked in blunt English what they were doing. They explained they were camping, and he began demanding a fee. Another soldier appeared and, talking more easily in French, my parents were able to negotiate a price of one US dollar to camp for the night. The soldiers left them.

The next morning everyone felt a little unsettled, and the group decided to move on. Frank and Emma—the other English couple—left first in their car, Mum and Dad following with the Swiss couple on the roof. As Frank disappeared down the road, my mother saw the first soldier from the night before striding across the hill towards the car. It looked as though he was shouting. 'Fuck,' she said to Dad, 'we haven't paid the camping fee.'

There was a split second when they could have stopped, but Frank and Emma had already left, and they were on the move themselves, driving away. They decided to carry on, leaving the soldier behind them, and they set off down the hill that would take them back to the main road. As my parents trundled down the long zigzagging road, they heard shouts from the Swiss couple, and realised that rocks were skittering down towards them from the top of the hill.

'They were throwing stuff at us,' Dad recalls, 'and suddenly I was overcome with that horrible, sinking feeling that you've just made a really huge mistake. And things could be about to get bad.'

Still, stopping to negotiate with now angry soldiers seemed unappealing, and so they picked up the pace, feeling far enough away that they could still make a hasty escape. But about a mile down the road they turned a hairpin corner, and saw that Frank had slid right off the road and was stuck in the mud. Throwing himself out of the car, Dad rapidly explained the situation to Frank and set about hooking up the towrope, a procedure that had become almost second nature after so much time on the road.

After a frazzled and nerve-racking fifteen minutes, they managed to get Frank's car back on the road, and set off again. But then, as Dad glanced in his rearview mirror, an old black army truck came into view, roaring down the road behind them. It was loaded up with men, some of them hanging out the windows, bearing guns and other weapons. In his words, 'It was pretty fucking terrifying'.

The truck was flying down the road at serious pace, and

as it got closer he realised it wasn't going to stop. 'Hold on,' he shouted, as it slammed into the back of them, pushing them off the road and into the mud. Frank skidded to a halt in front of them. Soon men began piling out of the jeep, screaming, and slamming their weapons on the doors of both cars.

'No matter what happens now,' Dad said to Mum, 'do not get out of this car.'

He opened the door and was dragged out by the soldier from the night before. 'He seemed high as a kite, screaming in my face. He grabbed Frank and made him stand next to me, then pushed us to our knees, pressing guns into the back of our heads.'

Everyone kept screaming and shouting, Dad's pleas for reason drowned by the noise of it. From his face-down position, my father tried to swivel his head and make eye contact. As he looked up, to his amazement he saw not only the feet and legs of other soldiers, but also a cluster of tiny feet and grass skirts. As he looked around further he realised he was surrounded as well by a tribe of Indigenous Efé, none taller than 150 centimetres, standing with bows and arrows arched towards him. He spotted the second soldier he had spoken to the day before and began pleading with him in French, explaining the misunderstanding and promising money. Eventually this soldier began talking back, translating his French to the first soldier, who was still jamming the end of his gun into the back of my father's head. Eventually a deal was agreed upon and, shaking, my Dad extracted ten dollars from his supply of cash under the seat, the first soldier snatching it out of his hand, his chest rising and falling from the exertion of shouting.

They left them then, the Efé people—who, until then, neither of my parents had truly believed existed—piling back into the car, arrows and guns, the jeep roaring its way back up the mountain. My parents, Frank, Emma and the Swiss couple climbed, shaking, back into their vehicles, and drove in silence down the mountain. It was only when they arrived back onto the main road that they stopped, climbed out and stood with each other, no one saying a word.

*

I read all these Africa stories from my new bedroom, wrapped in my duvet now that it's so cold. The diary intrigues me, intimate and distant at the same time. Mainly it strikes me how polite Mum is, all the way through, as though she intended someone to read it one day. In places there are big gaps where she's obviously planned to go back and add in some story or scene, but never got round to it. I can work out where they were, in the gaps, but the specifics are gone now. There's a lot that isn't mentioned—no gushy reflections on how it was to travel together, to be married. In places, Dad will finish certain entries like the whole thing is a book or script that they're collaborating on. The soldier debacle warrants pages of his impossible handwriting, and I can see how the story—the spoken version, the one I'd heard as a kid—has been constructed from this initial, written account; the words and phrases whittled into something funny, an anecdote. It amazes me that this diary, which travelled all that way with them, packed in and out of bags, is here on my bookshelf. Held in my hands.

Somewhere along the way, I was conceived in Africa. I wonder what they talked about all those afternoons, all those hours and hours of driving in the car. If, even then, I was discussed—the idea of me spoken out loud, the two of them shaping me before I even arrived. The letters and stories will never be enough for me to see it, to have been there, to have felt the press of the air, the mud and the dust and the sea. They spent the last day of the trip in Cape Town, a whole year behind them. They were alive, and they were going home. On the beach, my mother picked up a stick, walked down to the water and wrote *honey tour ends* on the sand.

Sumner

When my parents returned to England, they were astonished at how little had changed, how easily they could sink back into a world of routine, of job interviews, Dad's secondhand suits dug out from where he'd discarded them in the back of his parents' garage the year before. At night, me growing between them, they plotted their escape.

They talked about New Zealand, the name bold on their lips. Auckland, they thought, until at a rugby game in Twickenham they met a visiting New Zealander in the queue for drinks. He told them about Sumner: a beach town in Christchurch, great surf, great weather, great community vibe. Their parents were taken aback—who would leave home seven months pregnant? Interviewing Mum and Dad for this book, even I was shocked at the timing.

But all they wanted was to leave again. 'It was pretty selfish,' says Dad, embarrassed. 'Horrible for our families—you were our first baby. I'd die if you ever did that to us!' In fact, I'm not sure Mum and Dad have ever been forgiven for this move. Over twenty-five years later, conversations with their parents back home are always peppered with, 'If only you didn't live so far away . . .'

I think, now that their own children are growing up, my

parents understand more what a loss their families suffered as a result of their spontaneous decision. Maintaining closeness with our UK family has taken active effort, many long flights and long-distance phone calls, birthdays and Christmases passing with photos sent by post. I've seen the grief on my grandparents' faces, another teary goodbye at the international terminal, worse now my grandparents are ageing. Each departure takes on some barely concealed significance, some unknown number of future meetings subtracted by one.

But back then, those kinds of goodbyes belonged to an unimagined, distant future. My parents rented a house over the phone from England, Dad making enquiries about the job he hoped to secure in the first few weeks of arrival. My mother was growing—or I was—bones taking shape inside her, skin tight over the watery throb of her womb. I would be born in New Zealand and then, after a while, they figured they would return home with another good story, just one more year out in the world.

They packed up bags of clothes, some baby things. They had no idea what they might need in New Zealand—a place they'd never been. Their parents came to the airport to send them off, and everyone cried. Suddenly they felt afraid, but neither wanted to admit that they'd gone too far this time. So they left, my mother sitting heavily in her seat, her seven-month-old baby pressing into her ribs and bladder.

It was 1991. In the bright, grey light of an overcast Christchurch day, they nervously approached a taxi stand and asked the man driving if he could take them out to Sumner via a place they could get some bedding. He dropped them at the Warehouse. My mother moved slowly about the aisles, trying to ignore a rising sense of dread, the knowledge of a huge mistake made, irreversible. As if in confirmation, I kicked her hard in the belly.

The rental house they'd organised over the phone was dark

and boxy. It also wasn't in Sumner but in Redcliffs, the suburb before. To lift the mood, Dad suggested they walk to the beach and get dinner. The walk took half an hour, and once they finally reached the restaurant they were so jetlagged they had to take turns walking outside while they waited for food, trying to wake themselves up with cold air.

They'd done it now. My mother's pregnancy was too far along to go back. They found a different house, wooden and light, and rented that instead; Dad got a job at the University of Canterbury's student health centre. During her days alone my mother walked around, waiting for me, knowing nobody but somehow deciding not to mind.

The guy at Twickenham had been right: Sumner was beautiful. But more than that, New Zealand was, with its wild edges, its unpredictable weather. Now, looking back at them, I am amazed at my mother's ability to cut her ties. She missed her family but she didn't miss England. She simply shed it, like a skin, walking—so determined—down the beach in faded old jeans with ripped knees and oversized jerseys, her hair tied back in a windswept ponytail.

One morning in Sumner, Dad hired a surfboard from a woman at the beach. Trying to find him later, my mother walked into the house the woman had been standing outside. 'Chris?' she called. 'Chris?' The woman answered, appearing from another room with a baby, a little girl with ginger hair. The woman was named Piera, and they struck up a conversation, talking about my impending arrival. On the way home, my mother found herself thinking about Philippa again, the friend she might have shared all this with. They might have rolled their eyes—husbands, babies—they might have moaned together about their days in London, when all they cared about were clothes and lunches and the long nights they spent partying. She opened the door of her new home, so far from those memories now, and pushed the thought away.

Kids

I arrived a few weeks later. I didn't cry—my umbilical cord was knotted around my neck and I couldn't breathe. In the telling and retelling, Dad sees this and starts to panic. The nurses fuss over him while my mother, momentarily abandoned, glares at him with all the venom she can muster. It's a funny story, because I survived. Because they got to take me home with them, afterwards.

Back at the house, I stare up at the two of them with dark eyes, howling. 'Something's wrong,' my mother pleads with her assigned Plunket nurse. 'She never stops crying!'

'That's because she's a baby,' the nurse says, and my mother thinks that she might cry as well. They love me most when I am sleeping; when I don't expect anything. 'I mean, we adored you, obviously,' Mum says quickly, after a long spiel about how much she hated having tiny babies. 'But, honestly, I just felt so overwhelmed, so out of my depth every minute of the day. I had no idea at all, not a clue what it would be like. I was completely engrossed in you, of course. I just couldn't understand why I wasn't somehow better at it.'

They were imposters, they knew that. But I was there, with an infinite neediness that demanded they somehow make it work. They spent their evenings nervously hovering over me, wondering what I might do next. They marvelled at my so-small hands, my bright newness. The held me awkwardly, frightened but grinning at each other. They'd done it now, connected forever through this person they had made. They named me Francesca Philippa.

They found a card in their mailbox from Piera, the woman they'd met on the beach. She'd seen my baby announcement in the paper—a tradition my mother had stuck to, despite not knowing a soul who would care. In the card, Piera wished them well, congratulated them. I grew pudgy and soft, screaming as they blundered their way through parenting. Some time later, my mother walked with me down to the beach house, Piera being the only person she could think of to show her brand new baby to. They put us side by side, their little girls, Georgia only a few months older than me. Later, my baby book was full of photos of the two of us: stuffing down muffins on our first birthdays, wearing matching sunglasses on the beach, naked together on the grass.

Eighteen months later came Finnian, neither planned for nor prevented, just arriving as though it had always been him, inevitable. He was easier—calm and practical, solid earth. Even then just looking at him made you want to breathe in and out, slow down a little. He had dark red hair but we shared the same eyes, our eyebrows heavy on our faces, black peaks for eyelashes.

Piera had another baby too, and my mother would arrive at her house bearing wine and babies, slipping into Piera's group of friends as though she had always been there. She started to love Sumner: the slow pace, the terribly stocked supermarkets, the harsh sun on the pavement, searing the soles of her feet. Dad enjoyed his work, and on his days off would pack us into the car for camping and fishing trips, borrowing Piera's windsurfing gear and surfboards.

We didn't know it, but we were waiting for Matty, the one

who would complete our little trio of personalities. He arrived the day before my third birthday, in March. We were halfway up the Gondola in Christchurch when Mum went into labour, and the next day we met him for the first time. My parents were in the swing of it by then, enjoying parenthood. If I was sensitivity and Finn was quiet calm, Matt was a whirlwind of feeling. *So much personality!* Mum writes in his baby book. He was elfish: white-blond hair and tiny straight teeth, a body that seemed to move with his thoughts. Like all of us—a trait inherited from our emotional parents—he felt everything, but with Matt it was bigger. He was prone to outrageous tantrums that went on for years, his whole body tense with rage or sorrow. He loved openly and intensely, people folding out towards him as though he was a sun.

During her fourth pregnancy in 1996, my mother read an article in the *Spectator* by Dominic Lawson. His wife had recently given birth to a daughter, Domenica, who was identified at birth as having Down syndrome. In the two weeks that followed, Dominic wrote a proud and defensive article critiquing the tests that women are encouraged to take during pregnancy, predominantly to check for Down syndrome. He and his wife had refused them, and they stood by their choice.

Lawson's argument was that the tests not only endangered the life of the unborn baby—one in one hundred tests resulted in spontaneous miscarriage—but that they encouraged the belief that a disabled child is better off never being born at all. An idea that's hard to argue with, when the vast majority of positive tests result in abortion. In the article, he wrote: 'One or two acquaintances have still asked us, "Didn't you have the tests?" My wife says she thinks it will be difficult to remain friends with such people. I think they are merely missing the point, although it is a very important point.'

My mother took this article to her mother's group. 'This is

why I'm not getting the amnio,' she said. She believed—and still believes—that, for her, the decision to have the baby had been made, regardless of who that baby turned out to be. Four children, the big family she'd always wanted—absolute chaos, infinitely worth it. My parents already had the name planned out for their third son. He'd be Rufus—loud and charming, with a wild streak maybe, solid and warm and laughing.

My mother remembers my father's face, the slow dawning realisation that something was amiss. Their baby carried away just minutes after his birth. The slight frowns from the doctor and midwife, the touching and measuring. My mother, exhausted and overwhelmed, tilting her head towards her husband, his eyes on their son. 'I can remember it so vividly,' she tells me, 'more than anything else that day. His expression. He knew something was wrong, right from the moment he was born.'

The doctor announced softly that he was going to wheel them to another room to talk to them. My father put his head in his hands. In the bright, empty room, the words felt explicit: Down syndrome, a chromosome abnormality. Disability. My mother stared blankly. 'Down syndrome?' she asked. Beside her, my dad began to cry.

Over the next few days and weeks, as the magnitude of what it meant sank in, my parents grieved for the loss of the child they'd dreamed of, frightened for the uncertainty that lay ahead. I was five, and had my first day of school on the same day he was born. I went to visit my new brother in my ill-fitting school uniform, skirt too long, buckled shoes cutting into my feet. He was in an incubator for two weeks, and my parents slept at the hospital while Dad's brother James showed up from England to look after the rest of us at home. My father, distraught, refused to leave my mother's side, and eventually the nurses took pity on him, wheeling a bed in so he could sleep beside her.

As always, Dad read through the doctor's notes he wasn't supposed to see. 'Grieving appropriately,' he read out to my mother. Nothing felt appropriate—everything seemed wildly off-kilter, out of control, their new son so very small, coloured wires spilling from his limbs like exposed veins.

He was a stranger to us, floppy and quiet. My parents didn't know if they could still call him Rufus—he wasn't that boy, the one they had spent so many nights imagining. But he was ours. Eventually, Mum and Dad brought him home from the hospital, terrified all over again. 'Why are you crying?' we asked them, peering at the baby, waiting to see what was so upsetting. He wore our hand-me-down clothes and slept in the baby hammock suspended in the kitchen, same as we all did. He would fall asleep next to Finn on the living-room floor, their faces together, their arms intertwined.

'If only you'd known,' whispered well-meaning friends with pained expressions. 'Known what?' my mother demanded later, in the refuge of her bedroom, stubborn and tearful. 'What would I have done?' It stirred something in her—an anger, pushing at the floodgates until love poured out. Rufus, she sang to him, Rufus.

In Wellington, my flatmate has a brother with autism and obsessive compulsive disorder. When I asked her how this affects their home life, she used the example of family dinners, where her brother will choose to sit close by but in another room, finding the eye contact over mealtimes very stressful. 'It actually sounds weird when I say it,' she said, laughing, 'but it's just normal for us, it's just dinnertime. And he'll shout his conversation over to us from the other room and we'll shout back.'

In the same way that all families have their habits and quirks, Rufus has shaped ours. We cannot watch a game of rugby without him performing the haka in front of the TV, alongside the All Blacks. At dinner, especially if we have guests,

Rufus will always make a speech, usually saying the things we all feel but wouldn't bother to say ourselves: 'It's so good we are all here together, I am so happy to be with you all.'

Rufus loves us in a way that's completely uncalculated. When friends ask me what it's like to have a brother with Down's, I can feel him beside me: his worried expression when I'm upset, his face peering around my door in the morning, carefully bringing me tea or toast, his fast jokes, his teasing, his pulling up the loose strap of my dress or tucking my hair behind my ear. 'Hey, my gorgeous beautiful sister,' he'll say when I answer the phone. 'What's up? How's Wellington? Don't tell me—you're walking?' (He finds my walking hilarious. When he came to visit me one weekend, he couldn't stop laughing as we set off down the road on foot, waving his phone at me and suggesting we 'get an Uber like real people'.)

'What's that thing I have?' he'll ask sometimes.

'Down syndrome?'

He rolls his eyes and sighs. 'Soooo annoying.'

'Yeah,' we say, laughing. 'It is a bit.'

Sometimes he'll get frustrated. He knows there are things he can't do, things he's missing out on. He wants a girlfriend; he wants to drive a car. But I wouldn't say he ever feels sorry for himself—it's not his way to agonise over things, to reflect, to worry about himself in relation to others. We love that about him, his reliable contentedness, his wholehearted joy in himself and his life. 'I love my legs,' he once said to me, proudly admiring them sprawled out in front of him as we watched TV, undeniably short and slightly stumpy. 'Me too,' I said, looking at my own legs and thinking about all the times I've wished they were longer, slimmer, somehow better-looking. 'I love my legs, too.'

But back then, no one was there to tell my parents how great Rufus would grow up to be, how loved, that he would change their lives for the better. It was impossible for them to know that, one day, we would call ourselves lucky to have him—that he would be exactly right for us. Instead people brought sympathy gifts, the death of a dream apparently real enough to warrant flowers.

From the very beginning my mother was his protector, his fiercest advocate. She worried he would get left behind, the littlest, that the rest of us would grow up too quickly and he would always be struggling after us.

'I want to have another baby,' she said, quiet at first and then louder. Another baby would put Rufus in the middle, kids on either side to hold him up and push him along. He would be cocooned then, encircled; he could stretch his arms out and be held. Dad agreed, but everyone else thought it was a bad idea. 'You've got enough on your plate,' my grandparents said. 'You're emotional and you're being irresponsible.' Piera and Jamie had had their fourth baby by then, only a little younger than Rufus. 'Are you sure?' Piera asked, knowing—as my mother did—that four was hard enough. 'I'm sure,' my mother said, and she was.

Rocky was born in 1998, one year and four months after Rufus. He was so comically large than he was instantly worth it, our friends laughing in delight at the sight of his rolling legs and arms, his eyes like half moons peeking over the round domes of his cheeks. And he was beautiful. People stopped to marvel over him, his light hair and dark eyes. He was the fifth, passed casually between the rest of us, fed by anyone, taken to bed by his siblings like a toy.

As Rocky grew, he and Rufus were continually mistaken for twins, two little blond babies slung casually over each of Dad's hips. 'Partners in crime,' reads the baby book, and there they are: Rocky and Rufus sleeping, Rocky and Rufus in the bath, Rocky and Rufus on the beach.

At some point my parents decided to stay. They missed home, Dad sometimes cripplingly so, his brothers still his closest friends. But they had settled in now, with the kids in school and a social circle they felt they belonged in. To their surprise, their kids had Kiwi accents—Mum would call our names and we'd holler 'YIS?' back at her, looking up from our Lego or drawing or fighting each other. We spent our summers at the beach, tearing around Sumner on our bikes.

It's strange to me, writing, how much of my parents' lives took place in England. I guess I've always known how long they'd been there, but I always think of us as New Zealanders. As my siblings and I grew older, we got used to never locking the doors of our houses or cars, swimming in the ocean after school, playing touch rugby on dry grass. As teenagers we drank until we threw up in paddocks at farm parties, and, as adults, we left school and dispersed between Dunedin and Wellington. On long weekends we would return home, catching up with friends and drinking beers by lakes or rivers, getting sunblock in our eyes and returning to university with tan lines from our shorts, mosquito bites studding our legs like freckles. We grew up with Salmonella Dub's *One Drop East*, Katchafire's *Revival*. We used phrases like 'real good', much to our parents' despair.

England was far away from them now, without them ever really meaning it to be. Life, in its roar of children, had already moved them along.

Tokelau

My mother is laughing so much she's struggling to talk. 'You could call the whole book . . . "Reasons Not to Go to Tokelau",' she suggests, before dissolving into laughter again. It's late, and she, my father and I are sitting around the table at home. We don't often discuss the time we spent in Tokelau— it's not that we didn't love it, just that the experience feels like a long time ago, the blur of fifteen years spread out between then and now. It's easier to laugh about it all, because in some ways it has become a painful thing: hard memories, clenched and defensive, bottled up inside the tight cages of our ribs. Tonight though, we begin to unravel them, our old stories memorised still. We play songs we haven't heard in over a decade. And, like long-forgotten arguments that have slowly become irrelevant, we are amazed to find that, strangely, enough time has passed now. For tonight, at least, it has become very funny.

I was nine when we arrived in the Tokelau islands. *The middle of nowhere!* my parents had laughed anxiously from our hillside home in Christchurch—three tiny coral atolls in the South Pacific. We had dutifully looked them up in our heavy atlas. Oh yes, I'd said solemnly, we'll be here: this collection of specks off to the side of everywhere, this place so easily covered by the press of my pudgy, childish fingers.

We had stopped over in Samoa to play out a kind of holiday, trying to ignore the weight of all the worldly possessions we had carried with us—everything my parents thought we might need for our great escape from materialism. We stayed at Sheraton Samoa Aggie Grey's Resort in Apia, a final taste of luxury before our journey to the islands. Aggie Grey's was by far the best place I'd ever been. It had a pool, a buffet breakfast, and the Cokes we ordered from the bar came in ice-cold glass bottles. Dad would go for a walk and come back with hot papaya muffins; we played endless games of swingball while our noses cracked and peeled, slow-roasting in the foggy sun. One day we ran into a couple of Samoan men doing haircuts out of a little beach shack. My brothers went first and then me, my thick hair cut bluntly into a savage bob that finished at my earlobes. 'Oh dear,' my parents said afterwards, which made me cry. Later, my feelings about Tokelau knotted themselves around my feelings about the haircut. I looked like a boy, as the local Tokelauan kids would tell me. Where was my long yellow hair? They would've liked me better that way, it was clear—a proper glossy foreigner, not a dark-eyed imposter with board shorts and a bowl cut. In hindsight, my intense feelings of isolation were simply the result of being the only white girl on a tiny Pacific island. But back then, my loneliness was wrapped up in the loss of my hair, which I can still recall lying in forlorn, detached clumps on the sand.

We met a young woman staying at Aggie Grey's who told us she worked for Beanie Babies. This blew my mind. Not only did she have a long, swishy ponytail that hadn't been hacked off by shearing scissors, but she also had what was undoubtedly the best job in the world. I swam reverently behind her for two weeks, envying her hair and her life and her nice black togs, while she completed elegant laps of the pool. When we left she promised to send me a Beanie Baby—something that filled me with a hollow dread in the months that followed. I tortured myself over it. Had I expressed clearly enough that we were living in—*ha ha!*—the middle of nowhere? What if she sent it to the wrong place and my Beanie Baby was returned to sender? What if I never saw her, or anyone I knew, ever again?

Each of us had reservations. Except, I imagined, my brothers, who were younger than me and didn't know anything. I aligned myself with my parents, considering myself to be more on their intellectual level. In my mind, putting up with the boys was a cross we all just had to bear. This vision of myself as my parents' confidante and advisor wasn't completely unfounded: because I was the eldest, and perhaps because I was the only girl, my parents thought of me as more grown-up than I really was. Now they look back, worried and apologetic, at the things they felt it was appropriate to share with me when I was so young. Marriage troubles, money problems, mental health—my parents would talk to me frankly about whatever it was they were dealing with. 'How did I think that was okay?' Dad says mournfully, shaking his head, when I remind him of something we talked about years ago. 'You were twelve!'

This openness is something I have resented and appreciated in equal measure all my life. Often I didn't want to know my parents' problems, some of which were too complicated and hurtful for me to easily carry. At the same time, I couldn't *not* know—our relationship has always been driven by emotional communication, something I am grateful for and couldn't live without. Aged nine, I knew why we were going to Tokelau. It had started because of Dad's blood transfusion—that infamous rugby match at age eighteen, the first game back after his long stint with injured knees. He'd been tackled, and in the thick of it had been kicked in the side with a boot, rupturing his spleen. He'd been rushed to hospital, where they gave him a blood transfusion, although this was in the days before blood was screened, and the blood he was given carried hepatitis C. It never came up at the time; it's a disease that's problematic long-term but which initially shows no real symptoms, or at least none that Dad was aware of. It wasn't until he was applying for New Zealand residency nearly twenty years later that it was discovered, a round of compulsory blood tests showing up positive. 'It was the 90s,' he said, when I expressed amazement that he was still allowed into New Zealand. 'I sort of just flew under the radar.' He started taking treatment for his hep C around the time that I was born. The treatment worked but a side-effect was depression, which in my father seems to manifest itself as a kind of despairing restlessness. He was due for another round of treatment—something my parents had been dreading—and they pinned their hopes on Tokelau to provide distraction, adventure and purpose.

Despite wanting to support my father, Mum approached the whole Tokelau plan with trepidation. Travelling to remote islands with a young family obviously had its difficulties, most of which she anticipated (correctly) would fall to her to deal with. Dad would be busy with his new role as island doctor, an opportunity that had presented itself after a chance encounter with another Kiwi GP who had returned from his stint there. Although he, as my mother was quick to point out, didn't have five kids under ten.

'Are you sure it will be okay?' she asked Dad, who had seemingly sprung back to life at the thought of finally being allowed to go somewhere so gloriously far away. 'Oh, absolutely!' he would say, in full spirits. 'It will be our great adventure, the kids will learn so much. We're all going to have an incredible time.'

A word about my mother: she is not the kind of person who agrees to something just because she feels she has to. Although she will refer to the whole episode now as 'the time your father dragged me off to Tokelau', ultimately we would never have gone if she hadn't been completely on board. While her idea of a holiday differs vastly from my father's, her idea of a life does not. She can't help herself—she has to push things one step too far, to do the thing that nobody expects, to defy her otherwise predictable role of 'sensible' mother, doctor's wife. Once, at a party, my brother and I watched her, out of nowhere, jump fully clothed into the swimming pool. 'Why did you do that?' we asked her afterwards, rolling our eyes. 'Someone should,' she said, resolute despite the rapidly growing puddle of water at her feet. In its own way, Tokelau was a mad idea, an impractical idea—and, as it turned out, a flat-out dangerous idea as well. But in going, we would be doing something outrageous, and that will always spark something in my mother despite any hesitations. Had she known what we were really in for, I'm not sure she would have agreed to the plan. But how could she have known? The enormity of what we were doing hadn't hit yet, even on our last night in Christchurch, when she had to say goodbye to all her friends. They drank so much that the next morning Dad practically had to carry her to the car to go to the airport. 'Goodbye, life,' she mumbled mournfully. But she would laugh too; underneath her moaning she was as excited as my father.

Our adventure really began two weeks after that hungover flight to Samoa, when we boarded the boat that would deliver us to Tokelau. My parents had no idea what this three-day boat journey would be like, imagining a Pacific-scale Interislander complete with a bar and some kind of a cabin. But once onboard the boat, there was instead a kind of free-for-all flurry among the island passengers, choosing spots on the outdoor deck. My mother watched in horror as woven pandanus mats, mattresses and sheets were ceremoniously unrolled, whole sections of the deck claimed by more assertive families, fencing themselves off from one another with piles of supplies, including chickens and pigs. My parents worried about the five of us kids getting seasick, and as a result spent a long time trying to decide where on the deck we should set up camp—although it remained unclear what kind of camp we could set up, not having thought to bring mats and sleeping gear for the two nights out in the open. Thankfully, another family took pity on us and helped set up some kind of awning, which could act as shelter against the hot sun and night sky. The other passengers on the boat were mainly Tokelauans returning from trips to Samoa. The boat only travelled to Tokelau once a month, so any kind of trip away was a commitment. Although we were planning to stay in Tokelau for only a year, it was still unnerving for my parents that there was no means of escape if it all went horribly wrong.

And yet while Tokelau is an island nation, its inhabitants, in our early meeting, did not appear to be particularly seafaring. In fact everyone else onboard the boat seemed to cope with the long ocean journey by simply lying down on the deck and sleeping for the entire duration, an unfathomable option for my exhausted parents. While I was nine, Finn was seven, Matt was six, Rufus was four and Rocky was three. We wanted white bread, cut-up carrots, hamburgers and spaghetti. At home we were sometimes allowed watered-down Just Juice, lemonade ice blocks or Crunchy Nut Cornflakes. Here, an evening meal appeared from the bowels of the boat—chop suey with corned beef, or some kind of vegetable stew that had us dissolving once again into tears while our embarrassed parents tried to compel us into silence with their eyes.

On the third day land came into sight, so flat on the horizon that it couldn't be seen until we were right up close. The Tokelau Islands are three distinct atolls—irregular coral rings surrounding lagoons—called Atafu, Nukunonu and Fakaofo. On each atoll, islets have built up, supporting vegetation and a population of approximately 1500 on a combined land mass of ten square kilometres. Some islets are only 200 metres wide, and at no point higher than five metres above sea level.

Fakaofo, the atoll we were heading to, is five kilometres in circumference. It has two main populated settlements—Fale and Fenuafala—and then a collection of other islets that form the ring. Some of these are deserted: tiny tropical paradises which in time we would visit for our island picnic day-trips. One was literally called 'Rubbish Island' and was, to our great distress, where everybody's rubbish was dumped. The idea was that this was an alternative to burning waste, with the intention of reducing carbon emissions and combating climate change. Rats would swim between islets, beneath the swarms of flies and mosquitoes. To my child's mind, the plight of poor Rubbish Island was overwhelming (littering, as I knew, was *bad*), and for some reason this remains a stand-out memory.

Tokelau is classified as a non-self-governing dependent territory of New Zealand, and so receives financial aid. As well as a Kiwi doctor, the ship we arrived on carried a load of purchased goods—mainly, it seemed to us, packets of Raro juice concentrate and kilos of sugar. A popular after-school snack among kids was Raro eaten straight out of the packet, tongues and fingers turned lurid orange. My father later discovered these imports were responsible for the prevalence of diabetes on the island, and were the reason many of the children's teeth had rotted away to painful stumps. As a Kiwi I felt guilty about this, sure that without the aid provided by the New Zealand government, traditional island diets wouldn't have been sabotaged by these unnatural packaged goods like Raro and Coca Cola. It was a limited assessment, but one that mattered to my nine-year-old self, who would happily preach right and wrong to my family in a way that now makes me shudder with embarrassment.

In some ways, the Tokelau experience was a leveller between me and my parents; we were all learning, trying to make sense of things, each passing day demanding we reassess our view of the world. On that very first morning, arriving on the boat, I felt distinctly that my head was full of things I didn't know. Everything seemed strange, even the smell on the air. I leaned into my mother as we stood, watching the little island grow on the horizon. 'Are we here now?' I asked her. 'Yes,' she said, her eyes fixed out ahead of her. 'I guess we are.'

This was 2001. There were no harbours, ports or airports, so tourism was essentially non-existent. There was not even a pier or a wharf, so disembarking the boat, when the time finally came, involved a precarious leap from the side of our ferry to a small tin dinghy, bobbing in and out of sight at the swell of the waves. This was our first real introduction to 'island time'—these little boats cruising in and out from shore at a leisurely pace, not seeming to mind if unloading the boat was drawn out to an all-day affair. When we were finally ferried to shore, we had no idea what to do but wait there, unsure if we had been forgotten, or perhaps mistakenly unloaded onto the wrong island.

Fale, the most densely populated of the two village settlements on Fakaofo, did not initially appear the pristine, tropical island we had imagined. Crammed with houses to slum-like effect, the islet had a dense, haphazard feel; little shacks made of wood and corrugated iron spilling almost into the waves, rusting tin dinghies lining the water's edge. The land sloped down into dried-out reef and, with no room for animals, the pigs had been pushed out there in makeshift pens, eating whatever they could find along with whatever scraps had been dumped along the shore. To our amazement, when the tide came in, the pigs would swim around patiently for hours.

The boat's arrival was clearly an important moment in the life cycle of this little island. The arrival of beer, cigarettes, food supplies and family members seemed reasonable cause for excitement, and we sat on the shore, bemused, watching the hustle and bustle as locals rushed back and forth from the boat to what must have been a shop further into the maze of houses. Tokelau has, quite literally, the smallest economy in the world, and the one little shop—as we would find out later—did indeed stock basic supplies, many of which would run out before the return of the boat in another month or so. Aside from these few imported items, the locals lived off what could be sourced from the land and sea.

We sat, waiting, with our embarrassing pile of bags and the windsurfing gear Dad had insisted we bring with us, despite the fact that none of us could windsurf. My mother could only roll her eyes and breathe deeply at my father's frequent assertions that she would be soon be 'whipping across the lagoon'. Eventually, someone appeared to tell my parents they were ready to boat them over to the neighbouring islet, Fenuafala, and the house we would be living in for the next year. We piled back into one of the dinghies and set out on what was to be the first of many trips between Fale and our new home.

Fenuafala is about three kilometres from Fale—a carefully navigated, tight route across the lagoon. When the beach came into sight, we were flooded with intense relief, even excitement, too overwhelmed to note the irony of wanting a third-world experience and then being disappointed when your island isn't up to scratch. Because there it was: white sand, palm trees, comparatively spacious and undoubtedly beautiful—this was the island we had hoped for. A long jetty stretched out into the lagoon, and just beyond it sat a house, its weatherboard walls painted light blue, only a stone's throw from the water. We were met on the sand by an impressively large, middle-aged woman who introduced herself as Manua. To our great relief, she seemed to know who we were and to be expecting us. Manua was the hospital matron, vast and formidable, wrapped in layers of traditional patterned clothing with her thick grey hair coiled and shining. She spoke a bossy, clear English, which she quickly employed to direct us towards the house ahead of us on the sand. This little blue home was to be ours—the best house on Fakaofo, worthy only of a rich white doctor making a fleeting visit.

Manua was a great relief to all of us, her commandeering presence so welcome in those early, overwhelming days. For my mother, there was immediate work to do—all water, for a start, had to be filtered by a painfully slow little jug. My mother remembers watching the water filter, drip by drip, as it slowly collected into drinkable quantities, only to be so quickly consumed in greedy mouthfuls by her whining children or tired husband, popping over from the hospital next door. She never allowed herself to drink the filtered water in any great excess, instead painstakingly rationing it, ignoring her own thirst with a steeliness of mind that reminded her she was, at least, in control of something. Food was a similar issue: the supplies on hand consisted mainly of rice and flour, although the flour was infested with bugs. 'Sifting' was something we all became expert in, tipping sections of the flour first onto a plate, and then picking out the bugs with our unwashed hands.

While the rest of us were adjusting to daily life on Fakaofo, my father was also trying to get his head around his new role as the island doctor. Manua was his constant companion and translator, showing him around and organising the day-to-day running of the hospital. The hospital itself was incredibly basic: one little concrete consulting room with a bench on each side, a little wooden cabinet with a few medical supplies. It was also Manua's domain, and she would have my father standing on one side of the room—looking as important as possible—while she stood beside him translating. There were some relatively fluent English speakers on the islet, and my father could see them on their own, but for the most part everybody spoke Tokelauan, and the consultation would be mediated by Manua. In general, my father appreciated this, but as time wore on it became clear that in fact she simply translated as she saw fit—especially when it came to anything controversial, like contraception or birth control.

As well as the consultation room the hospital had a ward, a larger room with empty window frames and about six old hospital beds. There was also a tiny and nightmarish 'operating room' with one large table, and a little storeroom with 'God knows what' in it, as my father said, reporting back to us on his very first day. He had brought over some of his own supplies from back home, although compared to what he was used to it felt like next to nothing. The island had power for a few hours each day, the idea being that it was enough to keep the handful of fridges cold, but this varied according to how much petrol was available to run the generator. If something happened at night, the patient would be seen by torchlight. And in an ironic twist, the injections that my father needed to take daily as part of his treatment were supposed to be refrigerated, making Tokelau—with its tropical climate and sporadic generator—one of the worst places he could have come to get better.

To my father, the whole set up seemed alarming, and it quickly proved to be exactly that. In fact, it was because of what happened in that first week that, on our return to New Zealand nine months later, Dad decided to study emergency medicine, never again wanting to find himself in a position where he didn't know what to do in a life-or-death situation.

My father was visiting a patient at their home when Manua tracked him down, informing him that a woman was waiting for him with her two infant babies, both of whom needed to be seen. Dad returned to the hospital to find a young woman with eight-week-old twins in worryingly bad shape. At this point in his career, my father had no emergency experience, and could only revert back to things he had studied at university but never actually practised. Nervously, he checked them over, and knew immediately that something was wrong. Both little girls were floppy, quiet and feverish; he could see they were dehydrated.

He began going through routine procedures—monitoring their heart rates, trying to get them to take water. One seemed worse than the other, he noted, more lethargic and unresponsive, although it was clear that both were dangerously sick.

Knowing that he was out of his depth, Dad asked Manua if she could send someone to run over to the little islet office and ask the local man in charge to put through a call to New Zealand. This was a possible but painfully slow process, and Dad had little hope he would be able to get through. But someone was sent off anyway and, while that was happening, Dad worked on the twins.

Within the hour, the condition of both girls had greatly worsened. Unable to locate any veins in their small, dehydrated bodies, Dad had given the girls a dose of antibiotics by injecting them in the buttocks—but had seen no signs of improvement. One problem was that he had no medical equipment on hand to regulate dosage, and so was going completely off guesswork. He had no idea how much the girls could handle and, as a result, was being tentative. While he worked, the extended family arrived—or the women did, crowding the small room, muttering amongst themselves as my father frantically dashed back and forth between the twins and the supply room.

To my father's dismay, the sicker of the twins seemed only to be getting worse, her heart rate speeding up, body unresponsive, respiration rate high. He knew she desperately needed an intravenous drip, which would have helped with her dehydration and allowed him to administer antibiotics more easily. This was a problem for a few reasons. One was that he didn't have the right equipment or the right sized needles. Another was that she was very dehydrated and, no matter how hard he tried, he couldn't find a vein. The last problem was simply a lack of confidence. Recounting the story today, my father says he would never be as hesitant now as he was then. He would be much more assertive—higher doses of everything, a needle in her neck. But that day he felt only indecisive, and afraid.

With no line in and this baby girl dying in front of him, Dad frantically tried to think of other options. He knew of a procedure that could help in these situations—he had studied it at school but never actually had to do it. An intraosseous line: an alternative, more drastic drip made by drilling a small hole into the bone, the easiest option in this case being the shin bone. In adults the shin is usually too hard, but in children the bone is softer. Today, in hospital, this procedure is done with very specific equipment—short needles, only long enough to make the small puncture required. In Tokelau, Dad had only very large needles, and no drill. The relatives crowding the room began a mournful kind of wailing.

Nervous, and with no idea if it was the right thing to be doing, Dad began grinding one of the large needles down into the baby's shin. Testament to how ill she was, she only whimpered at this, unable even to cry. To my father's great relief, he felt the needle eventually pop into her bone, and was then able to administer fluid and antibiotics. However, he still wasn't sure how much she could handle, and had no way of measuring the dosage he was putting in. He was sweating profusely and, as he waited to see what would happen, the noise in the room seemed to increase in volume.

She died as the sun went down. Dad describes, tearfully, the utterly overwhelming emotion he experienced as this tiny baby was lifted, limp, out of his arms and passed around the room, the giant, inappropriate needle still dangling from her shinbone. At that exact moment, a message arrived that the telecommunications man had got hold of someone at Starship Hospital in Auckland.

Down the crackling line, my father frantically explained his situation to the doctor on call. 'I think my distress was obvious,' Dad tells me, 'and the man on the phone was luckily very helpful. The first thing he told me—which was maybe the best thing I could have heard in that moment—was "Chris, the first thing you should know is that these kids would probably be dead if they were here in Starship." That was a huge relief to me.' The second thing this doctor told my father was to keep doing exactly what he was doing, but to do a lot more of it. Higher doses, faster.

Dad ran back across the sand to the second twin and began to set up an intraosseous line into her shinbone. Once in, he administered a much higher dose of antibiotics. To his overwhelming relief, her vital signs began to stabilise.

Paralysed with guilt over the loss of the first baby, and with things having calmed down in the hospital, Dad soon walked back across the sand to our house, where my mother was waiting with us, terrified. She had heard the wailing—which had by this point gone on for hours—coming from the hospital and, although she knew something was seriously wrong, felt completely unsure what to do, at that early stage trapped by her lack of understanding around Tokelauan cultural practices. She had no idea if she was allowed to go over to the hospital or not, and as a result had spent the last few hours in panic, trying not to alarm us but also feeling sick, so sure that something terrible had happened. When she finally saw Dad, they both became emotional and overwhelmed.

At some point that evening, Manua informed Dad that the burial would soon be taking place, with the funeral to happen the following day. Because Tokelau is so hot, time is of the essence, and she explained to him how they were beginning to load many of the little dinghies with people before heading out to the little island in the atoll ring that harboured the cemetery. It was quickly decided that Mum would need to stay back to look after the boys—a late-night burial too much for Rufus and Rocky, who were already nearing bedtime. Being left out was something that came to define our Tokelau trip for my mother: laughed at and isolated by the local women, tied to the house by her children's needs. While Dad worked, Mum was often by herself for long periods of time, desperately trying to manage us all under what felt to her like impossible conditions. Instead, it was decided I would go with Dad to the burial, so he wouldn't be completely alone. The tragedy had happened over the course of only one day, and Dad was visibly upset and feeling responsible. The transition from death to burial happened almost seamlessly. In a way it felt as though we were simply being swept into it all, suddenly finding ourselves climbing into boats, time pulling away from us as though we were dreaming.

It was dark, and the night was filled with singing and wailing and the sound of the ocean. People carried flaming torches, and in the black inky ocean our procession of boats looked like a trail of close-up stars. I sat at the very front of the dinghy facing Dad, who was wordlessly crying. I had no idea what to do, so as our boat moved quietly across the sea, I sang him a song I had learned at my school back in Christchurch, called *We Are One*.

> *We are one,*
> *we're a part of one big family,*
> *yes we are one,*
> *we share the same humanity,*
> *and I pray,*
> *one day,*

that we might live together,
in peace throughout the land,
we are one.

We piled out onto the little island, and the burial process began. In the time it had taken us to get organised someone had built a tiny coffin out of wood, and this was now the centrepiece of the gathering, with all of us standing around it. Soon it became clear that, among other burial rites—which we could only really observe, as no English was spoken—families or small groups were approaching the casket one by one and laying gifts. To my surprise, when it came to our turn, my father tearfully walked up to the coffin and placed his gold signet ring inside. While I appreciated the sentiment behind his gesture, this was also alarming—Dad loved his signet ring, which his parents had given him on his eighteenth birthday. His brothers each had one, and my mother was gifted one too, when they were married. It had been on his finger my entire life, and now it glinted up at us beside this tiny, dead baby in her coffin on the sand.

When I look back through the emails Granny sent me from our time in Tokelau, those sad, early days are contained in one short paragraph.

Dear L & R,
Terrible day here. Little baby twins admitted to the hospital this morning, and at lunchtime today, in a very sudden rush, one of them died. I'll let C tell you the details when he is here—I've barely had a chance to talk to him—but now, six hours later, the poor little thing has been buried. C is mortified and heartbroken. I feel as if this must be one of the saddest days of our lives. C went out to the burial, on a separate graveyard island, across the lagoon by boat in the dark, and now he is back at the hospital, and I can hear the

other little girl crying. It all is totally tragic and unbelievable,
and C desperately upset. I will email again very soon.
We love you and miss you and feel very sad.
Ex

The funeral ceremonies carried on over the days that followed, with long services at the little church on Fale. This required us to sit for hours listening to what felt like impossibly long sermons in Tokelauan, although thankfully these services were broken up by beautiful singing. The church was a powerful institute on the islet, and the pastor and his family were looked after by the locals, with gifts frequently bestowed upon them.

It was during one of these services in the days after the funeral that my father, to his horror, realised the pastor's wife had his signet ring stuffed onto her little finger. She displayed it proudly for all to admire: the doctor's ring, made of gold, now hers. My father, who'd fondly imagined that the ring had been buried with the little girl, was very upset, and after the service hunted down Manua to try and get an explanation.

Of course, Manua explained, there was no point in burying the gifts along with the baby. After the funeral the gifts were collected up and given to the family, and *of course* the family had wanted to donate such a special gift to the pastor. My father had no choice but to accept this news, and then had to endure the sight of his ring on the pastor's wife's finger for the remainder of his time in Tokelau. Years later, the columnist Joe Bennett—a friend of my father's from Lyttelton—heard this story and found it so hilarious he wrote a piece about it. Only then did my father begin to see the funny side of it all.

*

Among the carefully selected things we had brought from home were three very large boxes containing all the school supplies we would need for our year away. The idea was that our parents would homeschool us—some English was taught at the local school, but not enough that we would be able to learn anything new. In order not to stunt our educations which, prior to our arrival in Tokelau, had been very expensive, my parents loaded up with reading journals, maths books and a curriculum, and set about trying to run a school for us young Henrys from the large wooden table in our new home. This lasted all of about a week. Screaming matches, tantrums and chaos ensued, confirming my mother's suspicions that one of the greatest joys of her life till that point had been sending us off to school each day. We didn't want to do the exercises she set for us, and more than that we knew her secret: she wasn't a real teacher. We were horrible, and she was quickly fed up. After a week or so of debate, it was decided that we would attend the island school and, after a year, whatever we lacked in the education department we would surely make up for in enriching life experience. As it turned out, most of the time we were so bored that a lot of the school stuff got unpacked and completed anyway. I read my way vicariously through all the journals multiple times, although managed not to do any maths whatsoever.

The local seamstress was employed to make our uniforms—bright yellow and blue lavalava for the boys and a pinafore dress for me. In the photographs, Rufus peers down suspiciously at his ill-fitting skirt, which was made of scratchy fabric and—as my mother optimistically describes in her emails—generally had him feeling 'a little hot and bothered'. Despite the fact that Fale was vastly more populated, the school was on Fenuafala, and for us only a short dash across the sand. Each day the other local kids would come over from Fale by school boat, packed onto an open-sided barge with a rail than ran around its edges. The boat was always teeming, children hanging off the sides of it, hollering and yelling. If it rained, it was deemed too dangerous to take the children across, and school would be cancelled—although in our eyes it all seemed dangerous regardless.

One of the most confronting things about school, for me, was the use of corporal punishment. If you spoke out of turn or misbehaved in any way, you would be whacked with a wooden cane which the young teacher used like a walking stick, striding around the classroom, tap-tapping it on the concrete floor. It absolutely terrified me, and on the first day, having witnessed a boy younger than me being struck across the back with it, I ran home at lunch in floods of tears, deeply upset that such an unjust practice could be allowed to continue. My brothers and I—as the white doctor's children—were exempt from such punishment, but that didn't stop my outrage. I had developed a keen sense of justice, which at that time somewhat clouded respect for traditional cultural practice. Kids being hit with a stick—by their teachers!—felt wrong. My parents tried to explain to me that it wasn't my culture, and I couldn't just arrive and expect everyone to do things my way. But I was hysterical, and tearfully demanded that my parents ring Mrs Lapthorn, my primary school principal, who in my mind was equivalent to God and who I trusted would come over on a plane and then the boat to put a swift and final end to such terrible behaviour.

Although I never really got used to the stick—and continued to feel spikes of anxiety every time it came out over the course of the day—some aspects of school I really enjoyed. At nine, I'd been placed in the older kids' class while my brothers were with the younger kids. Nine was an age where the Tokelauan children were really beginning to get the hang of English, and one of their favourite activities was a kind of round-robin spelling competition. The class would split into two teams, and each would sit on opposite sides of the room, with everyone facing the blackboard. One member of each team would stand up at the blackboard with a piece of chalk, and the teacher, from the back of the room, would fire off English words to spell. They would keep going until someone got a word wrong, and then next person from the team would jump up and take their teammate's place. This went on until one of the teams had run through all their players, becoming the losing team. It was brutal and intense, one of the few times in the classroom where the stick was put away and everyone could yell and scream to their heart's content. A word misspelled would receive an angry roar from your team, overlapping with thundering floor-slapping and shouts of encouragement for the next brave challenger, rising from the concrete to take the chalk.

I absolutely loved this game, mainly because I was unbeatable. As time went on, the game changed rules until it was me against the rest of the class. The island kids would rise one by one to try and beat me, but I was unstoppable, steely in my determination to be the best. This was obviously ridiculous—the words the teacher would shout ranged from 'ME!' to 'BOY!', words I had been able to spell for years. But I didn't let the disparities between our vocabularies take away from my immense pride at winning the game. I walked out of there every afternoon like a champion, cheering ringing in my ears. The only time I was ever beaten was when the teacher shouted 'NECK!' I immediately put my chalk to the board, ready to whip out another word, but soon realised I had no idea how to spell it. 'NEK,' I tried, to which the teacher jumped to his feet, shouting 'WRONG!' with breathless excitement. The kids all started screaming with delight, but their representative was struggling with 'NECK' as well, so then it became a race. I knew it had a K in it. 'KNEK,' I tried again, feeling panic rising in my throat. 'WRONG!' the teacher gasped, his foot hopping up and down on the floor. To be fair, I'd been on a winning streak for weeks, and everyone wanted to see me go down. In the end I gave up, and so did the other kid. Only the teacher knew how to spell NECK, which he proceeded to scrawl across the board triumphantly.

If any more evidence is needed that I was horribly precocious and a suck-up, it can be found in the emails I sent to my grandmother during our time in Tokelau. I loved using different fonts and would change font sizes and colours with headache-inducing frequency throughout my emails. I also had a tendency to describe everything as 'wonderful' or 'jolly'. I would like to think this was a result of my reading too much Enid Blyton, but in reality I thought it made me sound more impressive.

Dearest Granny,

How lovey that doll sounds! No shoes? How awful and in the frezzing cold English weather too!

Granny, are the baby doll's eyes always shut, or do they open?

Yes, dear Granny, we do have a fax machine, but no one can send to us (the mystery is some reason belonging to Dad). But we can send them—isn't that depressing!

Guess what Granny, we have a tiny baby turtle, about 5 cm long and about 3 cm wide. It was born sometime last night and it is black with some white on its head, and fins and a tail. I wish I could show you its sweet little face!

We are going to keep it until it is big and strong and then set it free—free to see the ocean and get married and have new turtle's with black and white on their heads and so on.

Well, I will leave you in peace.

Love Chessie xxxxx

I don't know why my parents allowed me to write these emails.

Despite my many irritating qualities, I was quick to make friends. Even with the language barrier, I found that I was able to communicate in the easy way that children can, and I spent much of my time absorbed in games with the local kids. Before long, my brothers and I began catching the school boat back to Fale when the day was done, to play until the sun went down and Dad came to collect us in our little tin dinghy. However, my new life was still pretty overwhelming, and I was a sensitive kid. Often I would become convinced that the island children were making fun of me in a language I couldn't understand. Back at the house I cried a lot, feeling isolated and lonely, pleading with my mother to take us back to New Zealand, where I knew my friends would welcome me with open arms. I pined for them—for our easy laughs and games, for the sleepovers and sense of absolute belonging. Now, my brothers were my only allies. Despite the fact I had spent most of my life bossing them around, they still allowed me to play with them, and the five of us spent hours entertaining each other. With no toys we mainly roamed around outside, climbing trees or inventing extravagant plays which I organised and then forced the boys to perform to our parents. There was one tree in particular—a large breadfruit outside our house. After the first few months we could climb up and down it like monkeys, instinctively knowing where the next slippery foothold would be as we swung from its branches. When I think about that tree, I can still feel its smooth bark passing under my palms.

To our great surprise, over the course of our first few weeks Rufus had become some kind of island celebrity. The Tokelauan people seemed to absolutely love him, many arriving at the house to play with him for hours at a time, calling out to him whenever he plodded around the island on his little toddler legs. It seemed to us that they recognised his disability, and responded to it with a fierce and absolute love that we had never experienced. He, too, met their kindness with nothing but love of his own, sitting placidly for hours in the laps of the island women or even casually strolling about hand in hand with the most impressive and intimidating of the island leaders. We laughed at how, compared to the rest of us, Rufus was able to relax completely, never questioning his place or worrying about whether or not he belonged. For my parents, who at that stage still had been keenly feeling the loss of the child they might have had, watching Rufus in this setting was like seeing him through new eyes. He was favoured, with no explanation, far above the rest of their children. The locals just loved him, his disability never brought up in conversation with the tactful but pitying voices my parents had become so accustomed to back home. This, more than anything else in those first few weeks, made the entire trip feel completely worth it.

When Dad had days off work we would boat over to the surrounding islets for all-day picnics, catching fish and then cooking them right there on the sand. We would sit in the shallow water for hours, eating and laughing, getting up to run races along the beach. Under the sea an untouched, pristine world of coral was waiting for us, and we explored it endlessly with our masks and snorkels. At the edges of the atoll, where the reef finished, lay deep water and danger. We had heard stories about fishermen heading outside the reef on the hunt for bigger fish, only to have their boats break down— catastrophic, as the likelihood of rescue was next to nothing. Beyond the reef the waves got wilder, and sharks laid claim over their hunting grounds. But in the safety of the lagoon we had free reign, marvelling at the teeming wildlife, a landscape drenched in colour as soon as you donned your mask. We saw starfish, turtles, manta rays. Huge tuna and trevally, the biggest fish we'd ever seen. Clownfish, angelfish, parrotfish. The coral was vivid, cartoon-like, scraping our feet as we pushed away from it. A few times we saw reef sharks, which we avoided. More than anything, the water was where we passed time, our skin gradually turning a deep, dark brown from days and days in the sun.

We were out on the reef one day, following fish around, when some of the islanders in a nearby boat started yelling at us. My parents were confused at first, calling back to the fisherman, asking them what the problem was. It could have been anything—often Manua would sternly tell off my father for allowing us kids to go swimming on various religious holidays, which were supposed to be spent inside (always news to us). That day we were all in the water, swimming in the same area but not together. I was further off, watching a group of parrotfish play games with one another, singing to myself in a distorted muffle through my snorkel. I heard the yelling and surfaced to see the fisherman in animated conversation with my parents. I watched them for a moment and then went back under, still absorbed by the parrotfish. I was disturbed a few minutes later by my father, who appeared behind me in the boat and hauled me into it along with the rest of my family. Finn was lying in the back, unconscious. As I stared at him he came to, moaning and shaking. He had just turned eight, but even then his body was muscular and solid, despite all the weight we had lost. On the floor of the tin boat he suddenly seemed very small, and my parents terse and frantic. Mum clutched on to him as we sped back over the lagoon, the boat behind us following.

It turned out he'd been stung by a box jellyfish—also known as sea wasps, they are considered one of the world's most venomous creatures. The sting from a box jellyfish is sometimes called a 'sucker punch': the sting can go undetected for up to thirty minutes after the venom has been well and truly injected, and the jellyfish are mostly transparent. While some people have died from coming into contact with them, most simply go into shock and experience a terrible burning pain and itchiness. Finn had been stung on the back, and welts were now rising out of his skin in protest. Dad carried him out of the water and onto the sand, heading straight for the hospital.

Finn's encounter with the jellyfish earned him some warranted respect from the locals. While I would have sobbed and demanded pity for weeks, Finn was resolute; after his initial screams of pain, he fell mostly silent, moaning and muttering but not overtly causing a fuss. He has always been the toughest of us siblings mentally—the hardest worker, the guy who never gives up. Later, when they were much older, both Finn and Matt played rugby in Dunedin. Finn was captain, and Matt once described to me the feeling of watching Finn in the changing room before a game, the team standing in a circle while Finn lapped around them, rarking them up. No one could push the boys like Finn could—he's a genuine born leader, the most fiercely moral guy I know. He's the kind of guy who, as a ship captain, would go down with it if he felt it was the right thing to do. He's a hundred percent in, always. Matt said that, in the changing room, the vibe would shift as soon as he started talking. He didn't need to tell me; everyone in our family knows what Finn is like, absolutely committed to whatever he's doing. Even as a friend he's like that, and certainly as a brother. He'll give you his time and his energy without question, jump to your defence and be on your side no matter what you've done. Whenever I'm upset or confused, Finn is the guy I call—not for his sympathy, but for his non-judgemental ear and unwavering love. It's impossible not to see the Finn I know today in the Finn he was then, a little kid with a serious jellyfish sting, uncomplaining and totally staunch.

The jellyfish sting was only one in a series of medical dramas that affected our family. The next near-disaster came not from the sea but from the sky, in the form of dengue fever. Dengue fever is a painful and debilitating disease transmitted by mosquitoes carrying any one of the four strands of the virus. My father, who had once contracted the disease in Tahiti while sailing, was immune, but the remaining six of us went down hard. Beset by fever, headaches, muscle and joint pain, extreme fatigue and vomiting, we spent two weeks bedridden, dragging our mattresses into the lounge so we could lie together in mutual fever and pain. My mother was as sick as the rest of us, unable to lift herself from bed to carry us to the bathroom as we vomited. Instead we surrounded ourselves with buckets in the hot room, opening the windows to try and create some kind of airflow. It was a grim scene, and my father would run back and forth between our house and the hospital, managing the water filtering and monitoring our illness.

The onset of our dengue fever sparked a rare email from Dad—usually Mum was in charge of the laptop, mainly because she was a faster typer and a more natural writer.

Hi all,

A boring note from the two-finger typist, as the rest of the family are laid out with high fever, joint pains and D & V. Wonderful. Seems ominously like Dengue Fever, but I await blood tests sent on last boat.

We recently had a telecommunications upgrade with the net result that the satellite link is even slower for us to receive stuff. One problem is that if you write back by clicking 'reply', we get a copy of our own letter back that we then have to download. It obviously wouldn't be right to name names, but Tubes—thrilled as we are to hear from you—it took us 25 minutes to download yours!

But please DO keep writing as the emails are one of the real highlights of our days. Come to think of it, the highlights are coffee in the morning, getting some emails, and having a cold beer on the deck at night when the kids have gone to sleep. Did we actually need to leave Sumner? Needless to say, we have already blown our extremely flash, state of the art, 100w per channel waterproof speakers when on our romantic wedding anniversary night we drifted from sharing a bottle of Dom Perignon that we've hoarded for years (only because it was in a box—interestingly it is the box that stops you when you're on one of those desperate late night searches for any more alcohol in the house) to an impromptu outdoor party on the wharf.

Esther is halfway through writing a withering review of the place of women in Tokelau—especially since she had to serve me at the Father's Day Feast, a moment I will cherish forever. Ventured out fishing with the boys yesterday and caught two great Trevally within sight of the house. This was thanks to Richard Sinke's specially made saltwater fly sent out by Erik, so thanks for that boys.

E here now!! I have dragged myself from bed to laptop to write something about the father's day celebrations a couple of weeks ago, which C referred to. Amazing church service with everyone immaculately turned out in white. All the men filed down the middle of the church after the women had gone in, and were presented with leis made of sweets, and fans and presents, which is all taken very seriously and was quite moving. Beautiful singing—very formal. Anyway, following the service we had the Father's Day Breakfast Feast (corned beef and sweet cakes) followed by protracted speeches, followed by protracted preparations for the cricket game. I was asked to join the 'serving women' who trail up and down in a half bow, giving out enormous platters of said food to the esteemed men, and pouring out very sweet tea for them. As C was sitting next to Pastor—head honcho, he got *an especially big platter—and an assigned serf whose one job it was to sit in front of him fanning the flies off his food. Anyway, Chris and she got the giggles because it was clear that he was struggling to eat anything at all! I just snarled at him in passing from my stooped serf position . . .*

Despite my parents' chirpy emails, our outbreak of dengue fever was actually a great cause for concern. Dengue fever is manageable if you have one strand, but nearly always fatal if you contract two. My parents were seriously worried that one of us would be bitten by a mosquito carrying the second strand—a thought terrible enough to have them wondering if they should in fact abandon our whole adventure and return to New Zealand.

Seems a terrible shame to leave now, my mother writes in her letters, *but we would never forgive ourselves if the worst happened.*

A flurry of emails were sent between Mum and Dad, their friends and family, and various researchers in New Zealand, trying to establish what strands of the infection were in the Pacific at the time. Eventually it was decided that we were probably safe, with only one strand known in our area, and would just have to ride it out. However, as the rest of us slowly, gradually improved, Rocky seemed only to get worse. At three years old he was already little, but by the third week of fever he seemed almost skeletal, unable to walk or move around. He was disarmingly quiet and still, leaving his mattress only to be carried to the bathroom or outside for fresh air. In the middle of the third week it was established that he had lost a full third of his initial body weight and offered no signs of improving.

During this whole dengue fever experience, our isolation began to sink in. The supply boat wasn't due to turn up for weeks, and even then it would still require a three-day journey by sea to get to Samoa. There was no emergency helicopter, no ambulance. There was no way off the island at all, and my parents were beginning to understand the magnitude of this. Desperate for help, they asked one of the island women, known for practising traditional medicine, to make a house visit. She arrived and surveyed the vomit-bucket scene, settling down next to Rocky. Still in the swirl of his fever, he could only manage to look up at her as she set about massaging his tiny body, talking to him in her language while my parents looked on. Thankfully these massage sessions seemed to make a difference, and Rocky made a turn for the better. The whole episode was the closest my parents came to packing it all in, and my mother had no idea if she was pleased or miserable when Rocky's condition was finally deemed stable enough for us to stay.

*

While some aspects of island life remained utterly unknowable to us—always the foreigners, always the outsiders—we found other things were mutually understood. To me, the only people to ever rival my parents' love for loud music was, in fact, the entire population of Fenuafala. Much of their music centred around traditional Polynesian drumming, but two singles tapes had made it there from Samoa, and these were played on a beat-up set of speakers seemingly around the clock at full bore. One of the tapes was 'Whole Again' by Atomic Kitten; the other, 'It Wasn't Me' by Shaggy. These songs had become the backdrop to all life on the island. I cannot express enough how evocative those two songs are for me of our time in Tokelau. To listen to either of them is to be transported straight back there—to the nights sitting outside, the sound of the local kids hollering at each other and the feel of my feet, with their toughened layers of skin, running over the coral and sand. In my very best memories my parents dance with us, holding our hands as we spin around on the beach, 'Whole Again' echoing out across the water. The locals would love it when we danced, screaming with laughter at my father, the doctor, grooving along to the music.

For my parents, who were often very lonely, music gave them something else, some time of their own when they could sit and talk and feel connected to home and the people they missed. They would stay up late for hours on our little deck, the moon throwing long beams of light out over the waves. They had brought a few albums with them to Tokelau, and they listened to them over and over again, each song a lifeline, something to grip on to.

I don't know what they were working through on those long evenings—how their relationship shifted and suffered, with no one to lean on but each other. Five children, my father's depression, the intense loneliness and difficulty of island life. In a way they were treading water, two people who had left home so very far behind them. They couldn't stop, or admit they had gone too far this time. It was all they could do to keep moving, to continue plunging their way forwards, hoping not to drown. But they did have music. For my parents, music has always been a balm to whatever hardship they experience—if nothing else, there is always one more song, played loud enough to fill the quiet. It's something they turn to even now, blasting their favourite tunes and dancing with each other. Observing them over the years has left me with no great illusions about marriage. To me it seems endlessly complicated, hurdle after hurdle thrown at random, the way forward so often obscured or hidden. When I think about marriage, I think not only of romance but also of the importance of finding someone who can cope with tough things in the same way you do. Someone who, if all else fails, can crank up the volume and dance with you, even in the knowledge that it won't solve anything long-term.

Not surprisingly then, it was the *hiva* that then provided a platform through which my parents could really embrace island life. *Hiva* is the Tokelauan word for dance, and when my parents were invited to attend their first *hiva*—which took place at a large meeting house on Fale—they were expecting the more formal, traditional music that they had so far experienced at church and during the funeral. What they found instead was raging disco, where the locals could dance to their heart's content, Atomic Kitten once again roaring from the speakers. My parents, in their emails, couldn't speak highly enough of these evenings. I think, for them, it broke the ice a little—a physical surrender that later translated into an emotional one, too. They danced into the small hours of the morning before climbing back into our little boat. They'd cross the pitch-black lagoon at full speed, no longer tentative about the narrow route through the reef. By this time, they already knew the way.

*

When September came we started getting emails from friends back home. 'Isn't it awful?' they wrote. 'Such a terrible shock. Those poor families.'

We hadn't heard about it, never saw the footage: two planes hitting the towers like birds, people making impossible jumps from the highest windows while the world looked on in shattered silence. It felt so far away: all that machinery and violence, the bright, splashing death. For us the day passed with barely a ripple, slow and sun-drenched, fish blood drying rust-coloured on the concrete jetty.

But once it had been called to mind, I saw that death was everywhere. When the pigs were killed they would scream, their hind legs bound with a rope, the rope flung over the long, smooth branch of a particular tree. Someone would pull down hard and the pig would struggle, its body lifted unnaturally off the ground. Then, swiftly, its throat would open at the blade of a knife, gaping in a toothless, bright-red smile. The pig would bleed out, the sand underneath it turn dark and metallic smelling. I hated these scenes, inflated intestines turned ripe at the water's edge. The fish, too, speared through the head by my aggressive brothers, flapping and gasping in the sudden shock of metal boat, burning sun. The water seemed so quiet underneath, and then here they were, the fishermen, probing and stabbing and ripping away.

And the people—their infected sores, their stumped teeth. For a while everything seemed to be rotting—fruit swelling and splitting, a putridness that wanted to linger, even as I closed my eyes in sleep.

One day I saw a man half walking, half running up the jetty. He'd arrived in a boat and was carrying a teenage girl in his arms, her head lolling with each step. When they got close he moved past without seeing me, and I heard the sound she was making, a dry moan, rasping and guttural. Her neck was striped with burns.

I ran behind them to the hospital. I screamed for Dad and he appeared, the man speaking rapidly in Tokelauan. He laid the girl down on the floor. It wasn't clear if she was conscious or unconscious, she just kept making the same raw, scraping moan. It was shocking to see her so uninhibited, rolling around with her dress bunched at the thighs. In general I viewed the young women on the island as ever-composed, often silent behind their husbands or fathers. I watched as Dad moved over her, checking and touching, his face so full of care.

She'd tried to hang herself—a cold fact, burning into me like someone had filled my stomach with ice. I thought of her hanging from the tree when the man found her, not quite dead. Afterwards, we talked about unsaid things, about not being able to see a way out. I cried into my mother, aware of the warm press of our bodies, encompassing and alive.

Going home

I can remember the first time I heard 'Going Home'. I'd been swimming with two friends, girls from my class I had become close to. I was proud of our friendship: they were both popular, and it made me feel special that they chose to spend their time with me. They would visit our house in the afternoon, playing with our things, giggling as they hugged my mother. If Dad appeared, or we heard his voice coming along the path, they would bolt from the house, shrieking with laughter as I chased after them, hot and bothered. I told them he wouldn't do anything, but still they refused to go near him.

Whenever my parents went off to a *hiva* I would stay with the girls, and as night fell we would creep our way up to the meeting house to spy on the adults. We found them so strange and embarrassing with their loose dancing, and clamped our hands over our mouths to stop from laughing. Once, one of the older boys found us outside the meeting house. He gave us each a nub of what looked to me like a sweet, dark red and cinnamony. We chewed, saliva sluicing around my mouth. After a while I started to feel dizzy. My parents thought I was tired when they picked me up, the wind roaring in our faces as we sped our little boat back to the safety of home.

Other days we would sit out on the sand, playing with each other's hair and passing the last of my precious butterfly hairclips between us. Head lice were rampant on the island, and I would half doze off in the sun as the girls picked them out of my hair, cracking them sharply under their nails until the concrete steps were dotted with bloody black specks, a little lice graveyard that dried up fast in the hot sun.

That day, however, they were annoyed with me. I didn't know why, and spent the afternoon growing more and more upset as they refused to speak English, swimming away from me and laughing while I shouted at them in Tokelauan to wait up. They were sisters, and it shocked me how quickly they could embody the language of closeness, an intuitive intimacy that naturally excluded me. They whispered in each other's ears and dissolved in laughter, their bodies moving through the water while I splashed, clumsy and close to tears, too slow behind them. Eventually I gave up, betrayed, sobbing as I waded out of the sea.

My mother was sitting on the deck when I got home, and she held out her arms to me. I folded myself into her, still wet, and cried. It was the intensity of my homesickness; the overwhelming unfairness at being held at arm's length by an unfamiliar language, by all the life that had played out here before I ever arrived. During my previous meltdowns, Mum had been relatively unsympathetic. Today, however, she entertained my self-pity, rubbing her hand up and down along my spine.

'Well, Poppy'—she still calls me Poppy—'I have a good idea.' She got up and moved inside the house. Pretty soon, 'Going Home' swelled from the speakers, loud even from outdoors.

She sat on the deck beside me as we listened. There are no words in 'Going Home', just music, but my mother translated anyway. 'It starts out slow,' she told me. 'You're leaving somewhere, and you're saying goodbye to all the people you met . . . you're thinking how sad it is that you won't see them again for a while. You're looking at the places you've been, all the memories you've made.'

We sat and listened. It is sad, in the beginning—the guitar slow and reflective over the hum of string instruments. I ran my hand over the soles of my feet, dry and tough as leather.

'Now we're driving to the airport . . . or, I suppose, we're getting on the boat and then going to the airport. We're watching it all pass by, watching the land get smaller and smaller. We're still sad about leaving but there's another feeling too . . .' The percussion from the drums had started, only softly, but I could feel what she meant—the beginning of something. 'And then you're sitting on the plane, and the place you've left feels far away already . . . and you're thinking about home. Because home is happening now! You're on the plane! And even though you're sad it's over, it's still such a huge relief. And, for the first time, you really let yourself think about how close you are.'

She patted me on the knee. I felt sad, for both of us. I knew that she felt lonely too.

'And now,' she said, smiling at me, 'guess what happens?' We laughed as the music kicked off, pumping through the speakers so full I could feel my heart swell.

'Woohooo!' she sang to me. 'This is it! We're walking through the airport gate . . . all our friends are there to meet us . . . we're hugging them, and they're driving us home. Through town . . . over the causeway . . . past Cave Rock, past Coffee Culture. Past the beach. And it looks just the same as always. And then we're going up . . . we're going up the driveway! And we can see the house again. There it is: home.'

I could feel it. My mother did a goofy jig in time to the music. The song was blasting now, drums and guitar, and we swayed along, shoulder to shoulder. Down on the sand the Pacific Ocean stretched away from us, blue and vast as far as our eyes could see.

*

When we did arrive home, it felt different. We walked around the house shocked by the size of our rooms, the elaborate emptiness. Soon our excitement gave way to an unsettled feeling. The walls between us were strange and solid. My parents let my brothers and me sleep on the floor in one bedroom, the same as we had in Tokelau. It no longer seemed clear where we fit, our lives suddenly lavish and excessive.

As I neared my final year of primary school, my parents found a house in Kaikōura, two and a half hours north of Christchurch. The house was solitary and small, tucked into a wild landscape between the sea and the mountains. The train tracks ran behind it, passengers and cargo thundering along them, a heavy thrum rising above the crashing of the waves. The house had two bedrooms, which seemed fine for the seven of us, my parents upstairs and the rest of us in bunks in the downstairs room. My father could work at the local hospital: a tiny rural operation, the promise of the kind of medicine he loved. As time passed, friends would come to visit, shocked by our lack of rules and structure. At night we kids would stay up playing, falling asleep on the carpet, the couches or somewhere on the spread of mattresses in our downstairs bedroom. 'It's inappropriate,' I heard a family friend say to my father once, picking up their small sleeping child from the floor. 'The kids need bedrooms.'

While our move to Kaikōura was definitely a ripple effect of Tokelau, we also hoped that a rural outdoor setting would help my father's ongoing battle with depression and anxiety. In Christchurch he had worked predominantly in the emergency department. He enjoyed it, but the hours and stress took their toll, and he had lived in a state of exhaustion, too emotionally drained to find room for the family who needed him when he got home.

While my father was struggling in his own way, by the

119

time we moved to Kaikōura my mother was gasping for air. With five young children—one with a disability—and an often detached and miserable husband, she was clutching at straws, trying to preserve a sense of self somewhere beneath the weight of everyone else's needs.

I heard her crying in the bathroom once, when I was twelve. It was one of my first visits home from boarding school, and I tiptoed away at the sound of her, my feet light on the stairs, heart pounding. It was easy to shut it out, like I did with the other things; their tense, indecipherable conversations in the kitchen over breakfast. He would put his arms around her when she was washing the dishes, and she would flinch away.

*

Whatever was happening at home, we were proud of Dad's new role as local GP. When we went into Kaikōura, everyone knew who we were. They waved at us in the supermarket, stopped me to ask me about school and tell me how Dad was doing such a good job. When I went to deposit some pocket money, the ladies in the bank laughed at how much I looked like him. 'And that's no bad thing!' one of them said, winking at me and then quickly backtracking when my face flamed red.

My parents enrolled my brothers at Hāpuku, a bilingual, two-classroom primary school with about twenty-five kids. Rufus started speaking te reo at home and obsessively doing the haka, which he had been taught by his teacher. He would stand on the seat of our ride-on lawnmower in the garden and perform it over and over again, not understanding the words but somehow knowing the feeling. The intensity of his haka surprised us, and when he came back into the house it would be with a hoarse voice, red welts rising up on his chest.

Meanwhile, I went down to school in Christchurch. I desperately wanted to go to boarding school—I had been on the school tours, seen the older girls in their uniforms and chipped nail polish. On my first night as one of them I lay awake, listening to the sound of whispered laughter and someone's homesick tears, the promise of adult girlhood now within reach.

When I went home in the weekends, Dad told me stories about what he'd been doing. It was full noise right from the beginning: farm accidents, car crashes, babies delivered in the middle of the night. At the little hospital, people would arrive complaining of coughs and colds, but after fifteen minutes of rambling it would be clear that really all they needed was someone to talk to—and now that person was Dad, the centre of a community he was only beginning to unravel.

One of his early patients was Sara Karl. She bounced into his office, age twenty, full of jokes and energy despite her face, which was swollen and aching. A toothache, she'd thought at first, but then it wasn't. Dad immediately felt his stomach sink. He knew that whatever it was, it wasn't good. He hurried her tests; she was surprised at how quickly he moved things along, giving her instant priority. It was sarcoma, a rare form of cancer.

Dad has often struggled with knowing how much to give, how to keep a professional distance, how to protect time with his own family when there are other people who need him, people who are vulnerable, lost, suffering, in pain. When we lived in Sumner, our neighbour Glen was diagnosed with cancer. Dad would go round there in his evenings, staying up late with Glen and his wife, talking them through it, Mum left alone to look after us. When Glen died, Dad had become so involved that he ended up helping Glen's ten-year-old son write the eulogy, standing beside him at the front of the church while he spoke about his father. In the months after the funeral, Glen's family moved in with us, too bereft to live in their own house without him. From a professional perspective, he shouldn't have let himself get so attached, so entirely led by his emotions. But how could he not? It was too real, too devastating. He cared too much.

Sara was the same. Dad grew to love her quick humour and sense of fun. She reminded him of me—not necessarily because we were similar, but because we were both adored daughters. During her months of chemotherapy, he would visit her outside of work, sitting up with her while she vomited or lay in pained silence. They joked together, she rolling her eyes at him when he botched yet another injection into her weakening arms, teasing even as she grew too frail to talk.

Sara battled her cancer for two years, and by the time she died our families had grown close. Rufus spent weekends with Sara's parents Jackie and Mike, walking Sara's dog and making endless tea and toast. Dad cried as he spoke at her funeral, and watching him I felt a profound sadness, a feeling that at the time I couldn't name.

*

Dad would often come home irritated. Compared to the intense stress and high pressure of his working day, the minute issues of our home life seemed unimportant and draining. By night-time he was exhausted, unable to find empathy for my mother's concerns or unhappiness. He would look around, stunned at the niggle over what had or hadn't been picked up from the supermarket when he just earlier that day he had told a family their father's illness was incurable. Sometimes nothing big had happened, just people all day long, talking about their coughs and colds and worries. He was constantly stressed, constantly tired. If he lay down, even for a moment, his whole body would crash—his face slack with sleep, my mother alone again.

One evening he arrived home at around 8pm, tired and quiet. I was visiting and the boys were all away, so it was just Rufus, my parents and me around the dinner table. Rufus was chatting away as he always was, but when he got up to leave the table Dad started wordlessly crying, tears leaking out of the corners of his eyes.

He told us that a woman had come to see him that day, sought him out especially for his advice. She was pregnant and her unborn child had tested positive for Down syndrome. She had a difficult and troubled home situation, and wanted his opinion on how hard it would be for her to raise a child with special needs. Dad had relayed his feelings honestly: that for him and Mum it had been undeniably hard, that Mum stayed at home full time to look after Rufus, that although we loved him, his life had never been straightforward. The woman, tearful, had decided to get an abortion.

Dad looked at my mother, his eyes full of heartbreak. 'How can I not take this home with me?' he asked. 'How can I sit across the table from him and not feel sick to my stomach about what happened today?'

I felt sick, too. It made me want to hug my brother harder, to rage against every word ever spoken that suggested kids like him shouldn't be born. I knew Dad felt the same way, but we couldn't pretend we weren't unbelievably privileged, with a steady income and a loving family. I went into the lounge, where Rufus was watching TV. I lay down next to him, and he stroked my forehead absentmindedly.

Falling through

Across the road from our house was an empty section of land—undulating, swampy, rising up into a hill matted with bush and trees. The trees were tall and overgrown, neglected, and covered in a weed called old man's beard. It had grown over their tops, forming a canopy that blocked out most of the sky, fractured light spiking through the knotted vines. From the bottom of the hill we could climb upwards, forcing our way through an opening in the beard and climbing up to the canopy, which would support our weight and stretch out across the trees like a blanket. It smelled sharp and green, and we would shout at each other as we crawled from tree to tree, breathless, our shins blotching red and stinging where we hit the nettles.

It was quite a drop to the ground, but we never thought about it—the weeds were so dense, and we knew the places where they thinned out. One day Matt fell through, dropping suddenly out of sight. Finn was beside him, and had grabbed his arm as he slipped. Matt hung, suspended for a moment, his legs dangling through the trees. Finn hauled him back up and we sat looking at each other with wide eyes, our hearts thumping.

We were close, the five us. When we were together I felt our physical presence, our strength in numbers. I was grateful to be the eldest, to have something to offer my brothers simply by having done it all first. They ran wild in our early years in Kaikōura, a habit of exploring developed from Tokelau. Collectively they were more ballsy than me, hauling themselves up one branch higher, paddling out to deeper water. For their birthdays they wanted things that felt so foreign to me: hunting knives, fish hooks, a real bow and arrow. But despite our differences, I could feel them looking up to me still, watching to see how I led the way.

*

Everyone tells me I look like both my parents. An exact split, I look most like whichever I happen to be standing beside. *The Henry look*, one of my friends calls it. Each of us has it. I know what she means—there's a straightness to our faces, dark eyebrows, the same noses and lips. Dad's green eyes were no match for my mother's though. The five of us stare exactly like her.

One summer, Dad, Mum, Matt and I got tickets to see Bruce Springsteen play in Christchurch. Dad always played Springsteen to us as kids, blasted late at night, the music bleeding into our bedrooms. I didn't mind falling asleep to whatever they put on—Dire Straits, David Bowie, the Rolling Stones. That summer, in preparation for seeing Springsteen, we listened to Kirsty Young interview him for Desert Island Discs, a BBC Radio 4 podcast. We were having dinner while it played, and at one point Young asked Springsteen about his depression. 'Oh, I've had to deal with it as time's passed on,' he said. 'It's usually okay, but then once in a while Churchill's big black dog jumps up and bites you in the ass for a little while.'

I looked up at Dad, listening, his cutlery held immobile in either hand. I knew he would be thinking of his own depression. I can remember, when I was younger, Mum giving

Dad a copy of Matthew Johnstone's book *I Had a Black Dog* for his birthday. Dad unwrapped the book and held it in his hands. They both cried when he flipped through it, and we, too young to understand, asked, *What's this, Daddy?*, pressing ourselves into them as though we could push away their adultness with our hands.

I could see it happen to Dad sometimes—his depression fading away, the dog momentarily curbed by a period of light and colour. A full picture, the world revealing itself in fullness once again. Although Churchill is widely credited with conceptualising the image of the dog as depression, in fact it goes back long before him, weaving its way through European folklore, through Greek and Roman mythologies, and through a body of art and literature in which black dogs feature as omens of death or the devil. There's something about the dog that people seem drawn to—the companion at your heel, silent but there every morning at breakfast and by your side at night when you try to sleep.

If it upset me that my father had the black dog, I don't particularly remember it. I don't remember the times he stayed in bed; they blur too much with Dad on night shifts in the emergency department. 'He has to sleep,' Mum would say to us, 'because he's been up all night looking after people, because he's tired.'

Who were these other people? I wondered, tiptoeing past the dark room.

I preferred to connect his grief to the hep C treatment, just a side effect of some random thing that happened years ago. It was easier to think of it that way, void of any blame I could be a part of. And often he seemed fine, humming while he made dinner, laughing on the phone to his brothers. But as I got older—old enough to know, old enough to ask questions—it became clear to me that it was never just a side effect. Long after he finished treatment, the black dog remained.

Once, I asked Dad when he had been his most happy. He didn't miss a beat before answering: on his honeymoon, the year spent driving the length of Africa. Mum's brother Andrew had come out to visit for part of their trip—one of my dad's few true friends. They sat around drinking and laughing and fixing up the car. The three of them had laughed and laughed, he told me. They couldn't have been happier if they'd tried.

Often we tease Dad about his melancholy ways, rolling our eyes at his mournful comments. 'Thanks for that, Chris,' we say, 'really cheerful.' We love Dad for his emotions, for the way he wears his love for us. He's cried reading my school reports, or reading my writing, or making speeches on my birthdays. Sometimes he is so proud of me that he gives me wordless, tear-stained hugs, and then has to walk away to calm down. Once, when we were in the car, I noticed tears rolling down his cheeks. 'Dad, what's wrong?' I asked, a rush of worry from the backseat. 'Oh, nothing,' he said sheepishly. 'I just started imagining what I would say to you all if I had to say goodbye for good.'

*

One night my brother and I are walking home from a gig we've been to. It's summer, and we're still sweating from our dancing, although the sun has long gone down. I am just beginning to get cold, my dress damp at my back. We're walking through a park, other people from the same gig laughing and shouting along the path ahead of us. We are wide-awake: body-tired, endorphins singing through our systems. We are close, my brother and me, carefully holding a space between us for the things we can't say to anyone else. Suddenly he starts talking, the words spilling out of him. He's sad, he says, he can't shake it. He's tried to take control of his thoughts—something we've talked about before—but he can't get a grip on them. He's

127

scared, he tells me. What if it never gets easier? What if he always thinks this way?

*

I often find myself looking for families. Watching for the repetition of faces, for the pleasing confusion on the end of a phone line. *Oh my god! You all sound exactly alike!* For my nannying job in Wellington, I wait in the school playground every afternoon. One day, the small mother with the tall two-year-old brings her husband; he is six foot. I watch them together, like Tetris—the father is the shape that fits.

One winter I went with my boyfriend to his family bach in Banks Peninsula. It was cold and grey. Even the hills seemed colourless, wet rocks that had slid out of the ocean like tired swimmers, their spines curling back towards the sea. We walked along the beach, making tracks between the seaweed and low-hanging cloud. The dog ran ahead of us, barking into the mist. We were there for three quiet days, only once seeing another person.

That trip, his mum drove out to visit us for the day, and we went down to the beach to collect mussels. I walked behind the two of them, watching their heads bend close together as they talked. They are very similar—often she would talk to me and I would understand him a little more; I could see him in her mannerisms, in the way she talked and moved. But there were also parts of him that seemed nothing like her. The year I met my boyfriend his father had died, suddenly, and was buried in a small cemetery further up the valley. We had been there the day before, walking between the gravestones. He was a mystery to me, this father, a man I had never met. I looked for him in the gaps, in the quirks of my boyfriend's character that otherwise made no sense to me. Sometimes he would speak in a certain way, or use a specific phrase, and my mind would drift back to the man I had only seen in photographs. There were physical things too—possessions left behind. I studied them like clues: the record collection, the book he had re-gifted to my boyfriend one birthday. The old shirts which now hung in my boyfriend's wardrobe, material worn thin at the shoulders.

I sat with the dog on the shore while the other two waded in towards a rock that had been recently exposed by the outward tide. They laughed, fingers pulling at the dark green shells, tossing them into the plastic bags we'd brought with us. I ran one hand down the goose-bumped skin of my exposed arms, wishing I'd thought to bring a jumper. I watched the two of them, mother and son, their narrow, slim bodies working around the rock, their easy movements so in sync.

I don't know what we inherit from our parents, but so much of mine feels stamped across me, a physical likeness to reflect the fullness of their influence. I always felt that I was emotional because I had been raised by emotional people: talking right from the beginning, unafraid of tears or love or closeness. I thought about my brother that night of the gig, his worry that his sadness would never go away. Was it entrenched in us, to feel things too much? Would we always have to fight it away—the black shape at the edges, bounding after us, a smudge of darkness in an otherwise colourful scene.

*

My father comes to visit me in Wellington, sent up for work. He is oddly happy here, whistling, calling me from the waterfront to tell me how beautiful it is out in the sun. He likes the buzzing streets, the food, the vintage shops, the boats that line the harbour. He visits his favourite shoe shop at the bottom of Cuba Street and buys some worn Doc Martens. We bar-hop, plotting future trips to faraway places. The next day, Dad finds a quote by Patricia Grace carved into rock along the waterfront. He takes a picture and sends it to me.

I love this city, the hills, the harbour, the wind that blasts through it. I love the life and pulse and activity, and the warm decrepitude. There's always an edge here which is sharp and precarious, requiring vigilance.

Always an edge here. Sometimes I think about my father's black dog as inhabiting the space between two worlds, appearing and then disappearing, creeping up on us from the edges of the horizon. We can't hate the dog—we know him too well. He is sad and lonely, needing our attention. When my father casts him away, it is with real hope that he will never return. And then he comes back, demanding that we start over, making room.

I can remember forcing my way upwards through the old man's beard, clawing at it with my hands. It felt so freeing to emerge on top of the canopy, the sky opening up overhead. And then Matt and Finn—the quiet shock on their faces after we'd pulled Matt back up through the trees, wondering what would have happened if Finn hadn't reached out to grab him and stop his fall. It felt like he was hanging there forever, looking up at us. We still went up there, after, but not with the same breathless shouting. We could never capture it again, that careless, invincible run over the tops of the trees.

Dad sailing on the *Dreamtime* in the South China Sea Race, 1985

Wedding day, August 1990

Mum and I meeting Dad for his lunch break, Christchurch 1992

A trip up Mt Cook, winter 1999

Rufus and me, Tokelau

First day of school in our new uniforms, Tokelau

Matt, Finn and I waiting for rescue after a boat break-down in Tokelau

Our last day in Tokelau. Dad was out of shot, being carried away on the back of an old door after pulling a muscle in his back!

Dad at Farewell Spit, 2000

At the CTV building in the wake of the 2011 earthquake, Christchurch
Image: Stuff/The Press

Memorial at the CTV site
Image: Donna Robertson

At home in Clarence. Dad and Finn built this pergola for Mum.

Matt heading back to Dunedin after visiting for the holidays.
Rufus always hates saying goodbye.

Looking into the kitchen the morning after the
2016 Kaikōura earthquake

The Clarence River post-earthquake, snapped by Mum during
her evacuation by helicopter

Rufus orchestrating the celebrations at his 21st in Hāpuku
Image: Billy Lewis

The Fallen Gull Club

I was thirteen when our parents separated, and I didn't want to understand why. I didn't care that my mother felt lonely, or that my father was unable to support her emotionally, or that none of it changed how they felt about me. Nothing mattered but the facts. It felt like I had been kicked in the stomach: a combination of physical pain and blind rage. I was relieved to escape back to boarding school, a world of routine, mealtimes and lights out. My parents phoned but I ignored them. I cried myself to sleep silently, waking with puffy eyes and a pounding headache. My matron clearly knew, which also made me angry. She would ask me questions when we were alone and, to my embarrassment, I cried to her too— apparently an indication that I was 'coping normally'. When I was home one weekend, staying with Dad and still refusing to speak to my mother, who was in a world of pain that I cruelly declared to be 'her choice', Finn had a full-scale tantrum over a lost sock. He screamed and screamed, which oddly cheered me up. It was exactly how I felt, a humming rage so close to the surface.

My mother moved into a rental home, and then later another one. She had been out of the workforce for fifteen years, raising us, and money was now incredibly tight. I was too young to recognise her bravery, too hurt and confused to realise the lesson she was teaching me was a powerful one. Once, wandering around her bedroom, I found Post-It notes from one of her friends taped to the side of her bedside table. They said things like *We love you* and *Hang in there*, and would be in her direct line of vision when she went to sleep. At the time, I wanted to rip them down—anyone who supported my parents in their break-up I considered my enemy. Now I think of what my friends might write for me, if I ever had the courage to do something that fucking difficult.

*

I was sixteen when my mother found our house in Clarence. We were repairing our fragile relationship, for once unified by our dismay over my father's new girlfriend. She told me she had found a home: somewhere she could really live, a place away from the dark and boxy rental houses that had punctuated the last few years. She was working full time in a café back then, coming home to cook dinner, her hands dry and cracked from washing dishes. She drove me up to see it one day, just the two of us winding along the highway, the sea crashing spray onto the road beside us.

Half an hour out of Kaikōura we left the ocean and the highway, turning up a white gravel road that wound up through a valley. The hills were green, as soft and round as familiar bodies, dotted all over with weeds and flowers. In the distance, mountains—still snow-capped in the cool spring weather.

Being around either of my parents at that time would bring up the same competing mix of feelings. I was in turns defensive and furious, dismissive and needy. I wanted them to hug me but I wanted them to leave me alone. Our years of fighting had begun to feel exhausting and irrelevant, but then out of nowhere it could crush me so swiftly, the hurt and anger every

132

time I heard them argue, every time they upset each other. We drove in silence while I checked my phone for reception. I knew my mother loved this place, this house I hadn't yet seen. And she wanted me to love it too—I could tell by the way she pointed out the lambs, skittering on their unsteady legs across the grass.

We drove for fifteen minutes along the gravel road, river and mountains rising up to meet us. I laughed when we reached the bridge. It was huge, stretching solidly over the fast-moving water, wide and concrete. It should have looked out of place in this timeless setting, but somehow it didn't; it had an important job to do. As we crossed over it the river seemed to widen on all sides, the bridge cutting its way through this wild landscape like it was so sure of its direction, of who it was meant to be.

*

The little farmhouse at the end of the road became our home, and we spent the summer cleaning its weatherboards, putting up curtains and painting. Dad came to visit, fixing things, driving up after work in his old shorts and T-shirts, stopping to marvel at wild deer or make way for the farmers moving stock, nodding at him with their sunburned faces. I was afraid my mother would be lonely on the nights we weren't there, but she never was; her head was full of gardens and soil, and finally, *finally*, a place of her own. She seemed to grow fuller in that house. With each space she made, she became solid again. I hadn't realised how much of a shell of herself she had become until she wasn't one anymore.

Her friends came over to help her get set up. They would stay up drinking and playing music, looking at the sky so swollen with stars, the absolute quiet. They would stay for the night or the weekend, and some people became regular fixtures, often themselves going through hard times. Late at night, after my brothers went to bed, they discussed everything: kids or no kids, family relationships, heartbreak, sadness. I was always welcome to join, never excluded because of my age or inexperience, always listened to and respected. I saw how much everyone loved my mother, how funny she was. This was more adult, more experimental, than any of the partying I was doing at school. I learnt to roll cigarettes for Mum and her friends, practising in the car while we drove the fifty minutes home from the supermarket. One of Mum's friends from work was barely ten years older than me, and I had my first joint with her, spinning out while she played '1979' by the Smashing Pumpkins on repeat. Mostly I listened to them talk, hanging on to their expressions of what it meant to be adult, to be a woman. 'Hymn to Her' by the Pretenders was always my mother's song. We turned it up as loud as we could, and gradually I realised I wasn't mad at her anymore.

The previous owners of the house had left behind a seagull ornament, hollow and plastic with its wings spread, designed to be hung on an outdoor wall. It stayed where we found it—we loved its hideousness, its absolute seagullness. Late one night, when my mother, a couple of her workmates and I were sitting around the table outside, it fell off the wall and cracked one of its wings. For some reason it was hilarious. It had never been a remotely beautiful or nice ornament, but now it was also broken, a symbol of everything that wasn't perfect. My mother hung it back up, and suggested we call ourselves the Fallen Gull Club, a club for anyone who didn't have a clue what they were doing. I painted FALLEN GULL CLUB down the wingspan of the seagull and hung it back up again, where it proudly remained, lopsided and broken, for the entirety of the summer.

Mum and Dad still argued, but they were also friends. Dad sometimes joined in on our Gull Club evenings, eventually falling asleep on the couch and leaving in the morning, taking the boys into town to their friends' houses or to school. They were united in their parenting, in their absolute interest in their children. I can't remember a time when they disagreed on something to do with us—schools, subjects, whatever it was, they led a united front, spending hours on the phone to each other every evening discussing our lives, our losses or achievements.

Their separation was messy, and their friendship was messy too, figuring out where to draw the lines, how not to complicate life for us kids even when they themselves didn't have a clue how to make sense of things. Those years can still bring back memories of things we said that we didn't mean. It was a shitty time, a low-point along our long, undulating road. And, like some things eventually do, it passed. They never divorced, and in total they were separated for six years before my father moved back into our Clarence home. It wasn't big or monumental when he came back, and although we teased him a little, we let it be as they as they seemed to want it: quiet and without show. It was a relief, in a way, but by that time we knew we'd be okay the other way too, that our happiness as a family didn't depend on their togetherness. I'd learnt what we all realise one way or another—that our parents are just people, and they don't have all the answers or do the right things. They stumble along, good intentions and sometimes bad decisions, making it up as they go, hoping for the best.

Grand plans

When I first started writing, I imagined it would be all about Dad. Or that was my intention—I was hoping to pay tribute to him, to talk about bravery. I also wanted write about rural medicine, how much it demands of our doctors and nurses, the inevitable emotional fallout. I had all these grand plans, but when I actually sat down to write it didn't work out like that. Instead I could feel myself being pulled back to other things—memories from childhood, stuff from Tokelau that I didn't even know I remembered. It's weird, spending all this time on something that might be good, or might not. Every day I am faced with a new decision: to include this bit or to skip it? To say it with these words or these ones? Sometimes I feel out of my depth. I want someone to be checking on me, telling me yes or no with a simple nod or shake of the head.

I am relieved to escape from my desk (bed) for a friend's birthday. We rent a bach in Waikawa, ten of us old friends from high school. When we arrive we push our way through the back gate, weaving through the sun-bleached tussock to the sea. The dark sand has absorbed the warmth of the day, and we lie on our backs, our arms and legs touching, necks craning to look up at the clouds.

We know for sure we are adults now, because we've pre-organised a dinner. We even end it with affogato, albeit in a strange collection of rental-house coffee cups. Given that only eight years ago we were smuggling Smirnoffs into the boarding house, tonight is an impressive feat—we clink our glasses proudly. We manage to channel maturity for most of the evening, sitting in a circle on the grass cradling mugs of red wine, cheeks pink from the heat of the brazier. People peel off to bed until there are only a few of us left. We take turns at choosing songs, the volume creeping louder. 'This one!' I shout at the others when it's my turn. 'Promise you'll play this at my funeral!'

'Oh, god,' they laugh at me, 'someone make her stop!' But they all know the words, and we sing at the top of our lungs, dancing together barefoot in the garden.

Later we somehow make it up to the bedroom, two of us sprawled across a creaking double. The room is spinning. My friend is optimistically clutching a litre water bottle, as if that's going to help her now. We lie in silence for a while, cocooned in the dark safety of the little room. 'I'm kind of worried,' I say eventually. 'I'm worried this is turning into a book all about me.' She rolls over to pat me gently on the shoulder. 'That's okay, I think,' she says. 'It's probably coming out just how it's meant to.'

The river

The summer my parents get back together, we go on a rafting trip down the Clarence River. Our guide tells us the journey will take five days, mountains to sea. We will begin at Molesworth Station and be carried, buoyant, down through the hills to meet the coastline near Kaikōura. The days are hot, and the river is low and warm, sloshing at our feet as we balance on the red skin of our inflatable raft, our wooden paddles warm from white-bright sun.

Our parents hope this trip will help us understand more about the river—where it comes from, the route it carves out across the land we so identify with. On the very last day, it will carry us right past our own house, its pebbled banks only a short walk from our front door. On my jogs, puffing down our driveway, passing paddocks and empty fields, I often wind up at the river; stripping off my clothes and plunging in, legs shaking and hot skin smarting at the sudden cold. I sit in the little eddy—a calm pool offset from the fast moving current—and look up at the mountains, cupping water into my mouth with my hands. In summer we swim in the river for hours at a time, the boys throwing themselves off the jump-rock further upstream, catching the current down to where we sit on the shingled bank. On Christmas Day we dragged

138

our dining-room table and chairs down there, eating with our feet submerged in water, drinking cold beers while our towels crisped from being laid out across hot stone. Being at the river makes me think of my mihimihi—the way I'd been taught in primary school to introduce myself in te reo. In a mihimihi, your own name comes at the end. Of more importance is your mountain, your river, your sea. This made more sense to me as I got older—I belong to these places, they can speak for me.

Clarence feels like home for me, unquestionably. It is our hiding place, our refuge, with no cellphone signal, no close neighbours. In the university holidays my brothers and I laugh at ourselves, our easy transition into these Clarence creatures, wearing hotchpotch outfits and rising and sleeping with the sun. Other times Clarence will be full of friends driving up in carloads for weekends, gobsmacked every time by the road, the river—the knock-out beauty of it all. They set up camp, erecting tents or unfolding mattresses, a group of my girlfriends once sleeping in a happy, drunken huddle on our trampoline. I know I make more sense there, tucked away in the valley. As much as I have built a home and identity in Wellington, Clarence is at my centre, the jump-rock from which I spring.

We leave for our rafting trip from Kaikōura, driving down to Hanmer Springs then through Molesworth Station in a bus. The grass on the hills is yellowed-out, dry, dust billowing behind us as we speed along. When we reach the river we stop, unload, one raft piled high with tents, food, equipment and bags, the other for us. We climb, clumsy, onto its edges, giddy in the novelty of our new uniforms—helmets, lifejackets, wet-weather gear. The river pulls us into her quickly, holding our weight. We cling on to our paddles, driving them into the water and feeling it swell against our grip, propelling us forwards. Our laughter startles some wild goats. The trees sweep up into knotted bush, summer mountains still with their lingering smudges of snow.

Days pass. Each night we set up camp by the riverside, our wet clothes draped over the trees as though we claim this wild space with our only possessions. We light a fire and hold up our hands to the warmth, talk about home and how nice a bath would be. Mum and Dad set up a tent, but the boys and I sleep on a tarp under the stars. We lie together in our sleeping bags, me in the middle, two brothers either side. I am aware of the shape our bodies make, rising up out of the dry earth like mountains, a landscape made from the curve of hips, shoulders and blankets.

One day it drills with rain, our hands turning numb, water sluicing down our backs. The river hums with the noise of it, the rain stirring up sediment until the water turns brown. Rufus sits at the front, face turned towards the onslaught, shouting out battle cries as we roll over rapids. In the quiet sections of the river we paddle to keep warm, our faces pink and stinging. That night we sit around the fire and drink red wine from a cask, the light slipping through the trees.

I wake in the night to find my father still sitting up by the dying campfire, watching us while we sleep. I wonder what he is thinking about—his five sleeping children in the glow of the embers, their bodies rising and falling with their breath. Maybe he's thinking about his own brothers, a world away in England. Or maybe just how strange it is that he ended up here, in this makeshift bed somewhere along the Clarence River in New Zealand, so far away from the place he'd grown up.

I lay awake for a while, watching. All around me the night is full of the sound of the river, its endless journey from the mountains, bending and curving to the shape of the earth. Where does the Clarence start, we had contemplated the day before, hours to ponder as we floated along. Why does it start? How do rivers form? We all offered suggestions, increasingly vague variations of forgotten geography lessons. From rain, from mountain springs? Snow melting? The river in infancy, just a cup of water once, pooling on the edge of something. It would grow until overspill, a thin stream suddenly breaking off, cutting its course down the hills, morphing to fit whatever lay in its path. And now, here it is beside me, a monumental, powerful body of water.

I can hear my brothers breathing, the quiet push of air, a slow beat layered four times over like a song. After a while it merges with the water until, fading into sleep, I can no longer distinguish what sounds come from where. I close my eyes, and home is all around me.

India

It was dark when we arrived, nearing midnight and an oppressive thirty-five degrees. From the window of our taxi, I watched the streets speed by; the roadside draped with wild dogs, wet sores oozing through their fur. Our hotel, an hour away, had a black tiled floor and a dry airlessness, the air-conditioning roaring and icy. We staggered around, showered and fell heavily into sleep, my neck aching from where my head lolled about on the plane.

In the morning I woke to the sound of car horns. I had been travelling since March 2010. I'd left New Zealand the day after my birthday, and spent a month backpacking up the coast of Australia—a bleary, beer-soaked, sunburnt trip. I met my father in Sydney and from there we travelled onwards, India beckoning. We had decided to spend six weeks together, just the two of us on a shoestring budget with a two-man tent, no plans beyond the morning ahead of us and a vague hope of travelling north to go hiking in the Himalayas. I carried walking shoes, a sleeping bag, a small collection of my mother's old festival clothes—long skirts and linen shirts, a purple-striped sarong. We ventured outside that morning and ate mango, sliced in front of us by a street vendor with a machete. It was hot, the sweat on my skin turning streaky black where it met the dusty air.

I was amused to find my father transformed in this setting, raising his eyebrows at me in invitation as we passed street markets, food carts, dilapidated temples. He wore a headscarf that I'd never seen before but which he had obviously thought to pack, and as we walked he stopped to purchase a beaded, yellow-fabric shoulderbag. 'Are you a hippy now?' I asked him, and he shrugged, happy. How strange that Delhi—this chaotic city, matted wires looping from street lamp to street lamp, the crush and noise of cars and animals—could bring out such a calmness and joy in him.

We headed north, winding our way up into the snow and mountains. We stayed in tiny villages where women with chapped cheeks brought us spicy chai, both of us bedridden by altitude sickness. We hiked way up into the Indus Valley with a guide, sleeping each night crushed into our tiny tent with our monstrously large packs and splashing our faces with icy water in the place of showers. We ate boiled eggs, roti and spiced potato, we drank endless cups of tea and bottled water. The walking was difficult, partly due to altitude and partly because my training for it had consisted of beachside beers in Australian hostels. There were two other people in our group, a French mother and daughter—both incredibly fit. Dad and I made silent, pained eye contact as we watched them skip up steep, winding goat tracks, the two of us staggering along behind.

Our trip was seriously badly planned. We were travelling at the wrong time of year, arriving at either the very beginning or final days of the tourist season wherever we went. The weather swung from wildly hot to snowy, and to wet. We didn't mind that; we had no agenda. We skipped the temples and churches, elephant parks and organised activities, parking up instead in tiny restaurants and waiting to see what came out.

Still up north, we hired an Enfield motorbike, Dad driving

us through rocky, mountainous desert while I clung on the back, trying to take photos with his camera as we bounced along. We stopped at random, once getting invited to what we thought was a party but turned out to be a lavish funeral. We took a perilous bus journey to Kashmir, rocks skittering down the sheer drop as we wound our way over the icy mountains, the horn blaring our arrival as we swung too fast around blind corners. In Srinagar we stayed near the water and paddled a canoe up to floating markets, watching birds settle on the vast lake like a fleet of tiny boats.

We travelled south by train. At some point along the way we stopped really talking and communicated mostly in observations, our conversations revolving happily around food. We ate giant crêpe-like pancakes with spicy peanuts, and so many mangoes that often I would have to lie down afterwards, never learning my lesson. We fell into a rhythm of admiration for the beautiful country we were traversing, the openness of the people, the harshness and richness of life there. I watched as Dad's hair grew light at the tips, his skin turning dark from days under the smoggy sun.

In Goa we hired scooters and roamed the beaches, amazed by all the tourists' bodies spread out across the beach, so exposed after our weeks in the traditional north. We danced at a beach rave, drinking dirt-cheap gin and tonics while trance music pulsed across the sand, green and red lights swimming over the throngs of shirtless tourists. 'Is this your boyfriend?' asked an English girl with long dreadlocks, wearing just a bikini. 'No!' I laughed. 'He's my Dad.' He's the best, I felt like adding, but it would sound lame and she had already lost interest, her eyes flicking across the party as she sipped her lurid slushy.

We spent afternoons in a beach shack called the Shore Bar, playing games of rummy while Dylan's 'Hurricane' played on repeat. Dilip, who owned the Shore Bar, took a liking to us, and would grin from ear to ear when we he saw us coming, holding aloft two Kingfisher beers with slices of lemon—'Indian Coronas,' he proclaimed.

I loved those Shore Bar sessions, sitting in silence with our cards, watching the sun set into the ocean. Dad would despair of all the dodgy tattoos we'd see on other tourists. 'Look at her,' he'd say. 'What's she gone and put all over her thigh? Is that an elephant?' I'd tease him for only pretending to be a hippy, for still wearing the shoulderbag. He'd grin, green eyes and crooked teeth, holding up his beer to his cheek to cool it down. I felt like I was meeting the person my mother travelled with all those years ago in Africa: someone content and at ease, his best self.

While we biked around one day, I was reminded of a story I'd once heard about a woman who posed naked for a friend's photography project. She was so nervous to show the photos to her mother, but when she did her mother cried and said, 'I haven't seen your naked body since you were a little girl.' As the days rolled by I could feel an ancient closeness coming back to us—some long-forgotten, childish unselfconsciousness. Even at the time I was aware how precious those days were, sleeping side by side, dancing together, the same way we would have when I was a kid.

I loved seeing that version of him, that unfolding, so new to me. I could also see, with some sadness, that the further from home he went, the more himself he seemed to feel. And I knew what that meant for our family—always having to share my father with the dream that taunts him: setting off, sailing into the inky ocean, the potential of places far from the humble routines of home. Sitting across from him in India all those afternoons, I almost felt as though he was floating, an infinite sky above his head, buoyant, on a salty sea.

Christchurch, 22 February 2011

Dad recounted this story to me on 14 February 2017, nearly six years after the Canterbury earthquake which claimed 185 lives. For some reason we were in my brother's truck, driving the two and a half hours from Kaikōura down to Christchurch. I often struggled to pin Dad down for a talk— his hectic work schedule and general exhaustion made finding time for interviewing tricky. But that day, in the car, Dad was wide-awake and chirpy. He tied an old bungee cord around the steering wheel, strapping my iPhone to it so I was able to record him as we drove along. It was so haphazard—the incredibly noisy car, the dodgy recording setup.

I thought I knew the basic outline of what happened that day, but this was the first time I heard it in such detail and I was genuinely shocked. The events of this interview are harrowing, and towards the end Dad had tears rolling down his cheeks as he spoke to me. Initially, I planned to rewrite this interview in the same style as the rest of this book, but once I transcribed it, it felt impossible to relate in any way other than the interview format in which it was told.

A week or so after this interview, we went to visit the

earthquake memorial that had just opened in Christchurch. I watched as Dad moved down the line of engraved names, grouped together not in alphabetical order but in the locations people had died in. I traced the words carved into the wall with my fingertips.

> We remember: those who died, those who were hurt, and those who experienced loss. We offer our thanks: to those who came for us, to those who risked their lives for ours, and to those who supported us. Together we are stronger.

Chessie: Okay, that should be recording now. You can start. Just go from the beginning.

Chris: Right. Is that the right end I'm talking to? Right. Okay. So I was there, Tuesday lunchtime. On my way to a two o'clock meeting—it must have been one o'clock, or whenever the earthquake was. I found myself rather reluctantly at Riccarton Mall—probably double-parked. I was in the entrance foyer, and I was standing at the ATM, and my memory of the whole thing was that, out of nowhere, the machine moved two metres sideways. And I found myself sitting on the floor. I just fell down, because the floor had moved underneath me.

Was there no warning at all?

No. Absolutely nothing. It just moved—I thought somebody had tripped me up. One minute I was standing there and the next I was sitting on the floor, and the machine was about two metres away from me. And I realised, then, that everybody in the whole place had fallen over. And then within a second or two of that happening, the shaking started, and there were people shouting and screaming. And then bits of the ceiling started cracking, and falling down. Bits of that kind

147

of polystyrene . . . you know, ceiling. Not heavy. Things were really breaking, and I think a few of the shop windows were broken. But it wasn't that bad.

Were you feeling worried?

Ah—no, not massively. I mean, I suppose I was just thinking, okay, this is an earthquake. I'd been in an earthquake before, actually . . . in the Philippines, oddly enough. In a former life. So anyway, I sort of staggered towards my car, and I remember realising, afterwards, that I never got my money out of the machine. I had a sinking feeling I'd left two hundred bucks behind. But anyway . . . so I got my phone. Everyone there was sort of wandering around, all quite chaotic but no one seemed hurt. And at that stage I thought to myself, oh, you know, that was a bit of an earthquake but I'm just going to carry on now and go to my meeting. Which is kind of weird. But I hadn't registered at all how bad it was, really—it didn't seem bad. Anyway, so I got in my car thinking, that was pretty strange. Had a bit of a ponder: should I go back to Kaikōura, will the meeting be cancelled. But then I thought, well, maybe I should go to it anyway, just to see. I had the car radio on—you know, I listen to the national programme. And there was a news announcement to the effect of—oh, there's been a massive earthquake in the Christchurch CBD. And the announcer was saying that it was all badly damaged. And I was driving up Riccarton Road at that point, away from town. I thought, well, maybe if the CBD's badly damaged I should be heading there—to see if I could help. So I turned around, and started driving back in towards the CBD. And I gradually became aware that all the traffic that was heading away from the CBD, in the other direction.

Is that when you first suspected it could be really bad?

No, at that stage I still didn't think it was that bad. I thought I'd head to ED, just in case. I'd previously worked in the emergency department, and I have a good ongoing relationship with all the ED specialists because we talk to them on the phone a lot from Kaikōura. So I felt I could turn up and say, 'Oh look, can I do something useful?' But I didn't have a clue how bad it was.

So I drove back towards town, down Riccarton Road and past Hagley Park. I was pretty close, really—I got to the hospital within a few minutes. I drove around to the ambulance entrance, round the back of ED. And I parked— God, I don't know where I parked—and there was quite a lot going on: people rushing around, ambulances, generally a sense of something happening.

I went up to ED—to the ambulance doors of ED—and stuck my head in to see if I could offer to help. First person I saw was an ED consultant who I know quite well. And I said, 'Can I help? Do you need any extra doctors?' She said something to the effect of, 'Well, actually we've got more doctors that we know what to do with, because the whole hospital is in emergency mode.' Which I think basically means that all the patients are sent home, and all the doctors are put to work in emergency. At that stage, they hadn't really got any patients because it was early days, and no one had come in yet. So she said, 'We've got lots of doctors here, and we're getting ready, but at the moment we don't need you. Why don't you get in one of the ambulances and just see where it goes. Go and do something useful.'

Were you starting to feel on edge at that stage? Had you thought at all about people being hurt, or needing to go and find Matt? [My brother Matt was attending boarding school in Christchurch at the time.]

149

I was definitely on edge. But I hadn't thought at all about people being really hurt—and I hadn't thought about Matt at all. Though there was a sense that something really bad had happened, I guess, because I think the hospital had no power—well it can't have done, at that stage. I don't know if I looked at my phone . . . or if I called home . . . The moment it really starts to dawn on you that all is not well is when you realise mobile signal is down, the traffic lights aren't working . . . you know, when all the usual parameters for normal behaviour have suddenly gone. I still had no idea, but I was beginning to get a sense that yes, this could be bad.

Anyway, as it happened there was an ambulance that was just leaving, and so I knocked on the door, opened it up and basically jumped on in. There were two other doctors in the back who I knew—one was David Richards, and the other Stuart Barrington-Onslow. And they knew me—it wasn't like I was a complete random who jumped in. So I said, 'Hey look, can I help?' and they said, 'We don't know, but come along anyway.'

And as it transpired, this ambulance was taking us to Latimer Square to set up a sort of medical triage centre. I think it was one of several around the city. They'd already decided on some locations—I guess 'they' meaning Civil Defence, or this might have been some kind of pre-arranged emergency plan. But anyway, somebody had made the decision that there was going to be a kind of medical post at Latimer Square. We didn't really know what else was going on, because there was such a complete absence of communication . . . you really were in your own little world. In fact one of the problems later on was that we didn't really know what state the hospital was in, and had no real way of getting in touch. But in that early stage I just got in the ambulance and off we went.

What was the scene like when you got to Latimer Square?

Well, that's when it became pretty confusing. We were among the first to arrive, but there were several ambulances, some paramedics, some fire fighters . . . a lot of dust. Dust billowing up from the buildings around us. Some of those buildings had been quite badly damaged—there was glass everywhere. The Copthorne Hotel—a ginormous building—was quite obviously on an angle. That felt pretty odd.

It was all very confusing. And we were trying to organise it a bit—talking to the ambulance people, trying to work out a plan of action. One of the ambulance guys must have been in charge, and he was saying, 'Okay, so we're going to set up a receiving area here, and another area here . . .' I think they had some cones, and we started trying to make different areas.

Were there any patients at that stage?

Yeah, there were a few people sitting around on the grass. I was wandering around, kind of wondering what to do. Luckily I had a sort of high-vis vest, which I had grabbed from the back of my car. It was my PRIME [Primary Response in Medical Emergencies] vest, so it said PRIME DOCTOR on the back. At that stage I noticed there were three bodies lying on the grass, which someone had left there. Or I don't know how they got there. Someone was trying to put a blanket over them, or a jacket over their faces. And that was the moment it sort of dawned on me, you know, how serious it was. And, because I wasn't really doing anything else, I decided to create some kind of morgue area . . . to give them a bit of privacy.

Actually, the first person I really talked to was some guy who rode up on his bike. Literally came powering along on his pedal bike and jumped off and said, 'Can I help?' He said he was an engineering student, and so I said, 'Well, what

I'm trying to do is a make a morgue for these people.' As it happened, a building at the end of Latimer Square had a whole lot of tarpaulins over it for some reason—it must have been under construction or something. And so I said, 'If you're an engineering student—you must have a pocket knife! Why don't you go and cut down one of those.' He did, and we decided to wrap it around some of the trees in Latimer Square and make it into a little room. So that, as I recall, was probably the first useful thing I did.

But then people started arriving. It's hard to remember at what stage everything happened. There were some really huge aftershocks. Big ones. And the buildings around Latimer Square, they were moving a lot. You could look at this fifteen-storey skyscraper and it would be rocking back and forth, the windows popping out. Quite amazing.

It would be terrifying.

Well . . . I'm not sure that at any stage over the whole day I felt scared, really. It's sort of more . . . just being in the moment, what next, what next. I mean, we definitely felt at certain stages like, oh god, that could come down, you know. Everyone was trying to calculate what would happen. If a fifteen-storey building falls down and it's on the other side of the road, is it going to hit you, that kind of thing. And I think it probably wouldn't have. I mean, that's why we were in Latimer Square—it's a big park, you know. If you were in a street somewhere, it would have been different.

But anyway, by this time more people were arriving. And it was like a movie.

Like a movie?

Well, yeah. Ambulance officers started bringing people in

... either carrying them, or they were walking. And then people started dropping others off in cars, with people lying across the bonnet. Things like that. One person got carried in on a door. And while there was a lot of damage at Latimer Square—and there was—it was pretty obvious that there was a lot more damage about two blocks away. I later realised that was the CTV building.

The whole thing was very disorientating. There were clouds of dust everywhere. The aftershocks were noisy—there was a lot of crashing and breaking, things falling down. But mainly I remember the dust. All the injured people who got brought in were covered in dust.

How was the park set up?

Actually it organised pretty quickly. There were two stages to it: the initial stage and then a later, more officially organised stage. In the beginning it was designated areas and a quick sort of split-up of personnel. More ambulance people had arrived—quite a big group of doctors arrived who had actually been at a Paediatric Advanced Life Support course at the Copthorne Hotel. They already had roles established on the course ... course leader, tutor, participants. So weirdly enough they came down with that structure already in place. One of the guys already had a big badge saying leader, and he just became the leader of that group. But anyway, Stuart and I, and the other ambulance people, had done a quick divvy-up of roles. I was doing initial assessment—

What do you mean by initial assessment?

Well, so ... meet and greet, as we call it—a very rapid triage where you don't try and do anything, you just assess people, and from there send them off to the relevant place. So anybody who was injured but able to walk—you know, nothing too serious—was going to be moved on to the nearby after-hours. I don't know how that was happening, but it was. I think people were being ferried off in ambulances. Basically you have these 1, 2 and 3 categories. We didn't make these up, by the way—this is established practice. So, status 0 means you're already dead. Status 1 means you need life-saving intervention right now, like you're in cardiac arrest or something. Status 2 means you need immediate care—a crush injury to the chest, something very serious. Status 3 is injured but okay—you're going to be fine if you're left for twenty minutes. A broken leg, for example. But you have to be careful; you know, it's all well and good until someone bleeds out from their broken leg. Status 4 and 5 are the walking wounded, and they all went away somewhere else. This is standard triage: you do A, B, C. Airway—are their airways functioning and clear. If they're making a horrible noise, you'd be worried about that. B is breathing, so if someone is breathing really fast you might wonder if they have a chest injury or a ruptured lung or something like that—you're want to check that their breathing is normal. And C is for circulation, so you need to check if they're bleeding either internally or externally. That's about pulse and blood pressure. If their blood pressure is really low, and their heart is beating really fast trying to pump the blood around—that's when you've got a problem with C.

This was actually quite difficult, in the circumstances. At this stage we were just setting up, we didn't have much gear and we didn't know what state the hospital was in. There wasn't any way of phoning to check . . . we didn't really have ambulances available and there were lots of people to assess. One of the decisions that was made right at the beginning was that if someone was status 1—i.e., they needed to be intubated right now or they would die, or they needed CPR right now or they would die—then it was pretty clear that these people were going to die. And that's why triage can be a brutal process, because you have to ask what is the best use of the resources that we have. You have to put your effort into the people you think you can save. It wasn't an official decision—and I don't know how you'll write this in your book—but there was an acknowledgement, let's say that, between all the people who were there at the beginning, that we didn't have the gear, the time or the resources to spend a lot of time trying to save someone who was clearly going to die anyway. We felt it was better to prioritise status 2 people who we could save.

Did you have many status 1 people come in?

I think about two. Two people turned up as status 1, and then died very quickly. So that was pretty difficult.

Were you overwhelmed? Did it feel like an insane situation at the time?

Yep, it did feel very stressful. Particularly because on the move, on your feet in real time, you're trying to make sense of a whole different framework for what you're doing. I saw someone, I remember, who had been crushed by a whole lot of falling masonry, and had a spinal injury. Her ABC was okay, but she couldn't move her legs properly . . . you know, something that in normal life I would have thought of as absolutely top priority. And I was saying, 'Oh, I think she's okay, her ABCs are okay, let's not worry about her for a minute.' And Stuart said, 'Chris, that's wrong—because she has a potentially paralysing injury.' And of course he was right, and clearly we needed to send her off to the hospital—which we were quietly hoping hadn't fallen down in one of the aftershocks. And when I thought about it afterwards I thought, well yes, that was really stupid and obvious. But it's very intense, in that situation—you almost end up swinging the other way, thinking, you're not as bad as the person I just saw, you'll be fine. It was difficult. It was a new experience for everyone— and you're trying to make the right decisions, very quickly.

But this triage stage actually happened over a short space of time, and while initially there was a whole flurry of people coming in, after a while it started slowing down. Originally I'd been assigned to do the meet and greet, but after a while I was going over to see Stuart and helping him, helping at some of the other areas.

Were there many status 2 people?

Yeah, there were a lot of crush injuries. Broken limbs, spinal injuries, head injuries, abdominal injuries. A lot of people who were really badly hurt. And a lot of cuts, scrapes . . . stuff like that.

What was atmosphere around Latimer Square? I mean, everyone reacts to shock differently.

I think everyone was pretty shellshocked. Some people were very stoically sitting around . . . There were a lot of anxious people with nothing to do, pacing around, trying to find a role in it all. People looking for missing friends and family. The press had turned up, and lot of people were angry about that. We'd been told early on to be careful about who we spoke to, so I think we were conscious of that among everything else. I mean, these situations can be really frustrating . . . not everyone is trained for emergency, which is completely fair enough. And in the circumstances, I think it did go pretty well . . . but just certain things—setting up drips, for example. Some of the doctors and nurses who had turned up were trying to be really nice—and I don't mean this nastily—but, you know, trying to be delicate with the patients as you normally would, trying to put a little teeny drip in the back of their hands. And that's just not the right way to go about it in an emergency. You want the largest possible drip in the biggest possible vein, as quickly as you possibly can. So I guess there was a certain edginess about that—around trying to get a move on.

But generally I think the set-up worked really well. Some sense of order prevailed in the end, and the people who needed to go to hospital got there, or seemed to. I think one of the hardest things is to have any recollection whatsoever of the timeline. You completely lose track—the only clear point I can remember in regards to time was when it got dark, and that was much later. So that would have been . . . well, it would be like today, wouldn't it? Nine or ten in the evening. The whole afternoon was a blur, really.

Anyway, Latimer Square eventually subsided . . . and lots of doctors and nurses had turned up. There was an attempt to organise people, start a rotation so if someone was tired, someone else could tag in for them, that sort of thing. I think in hindsight we probably could have done better—we just didn't know what skills we had there. We should have said, 'Does someone here have orthopaedic experience? Is someone here an anaesthetist?' Because I think afterwards people felt—well, there were some army doctors for example, who I think had a lot of experience but had to wait their turn to get involved. It's difficult at the time—you've got people working, they're in a team, it's sort of going okay. It's hard to say, 'Okay, all of you who are junior, we don't need you anymore, we're going to get someone else.'

It sounds chaotic.

Well, it got criticised for being chaotic. But I think we did incredibly well considering that, for the most part, everyone was making it up as they went along. And after a few hours, St John—or it might have been the army, actually—turned up with these inflatable tents. Because initially these areas— these 1, 2 and 3 areas—were just bits of grass. And they deposited some gear in each one, and then there were these field tents, which created a bit more organisation. So there was some kind of semblance of order, you know, within a couple of hours.

But after a while we weren't sure what to do, because— weirdly enough—we ran out of patients, or at least, we had more than enough doctors, and it came to dawn on us that everybody who could get there had already got there. Either that or they'd gone to other places, gone to other hospitals—or had just taken off. I'm sure a lot of people just fled. Lots of people went to the after-hours clinic—and that was a whole other huge scene that at the time we knew nothing about.

It's so strange to think about that—a different dramatic scene happening somewhere else.

Yeah, and we knew nothing about it. We had no communication with the hospital, no idea about the after-hours.

Had you thought about Matt yet?

Yes. I mean, I knew that he was in the CBD, at school. I had tried to call him, and to call home, but the phone lines weren't working. And because I couldn't call him, and I couldn't leave . . . there wasn't really much I could do about it.

Did you feel like you couldn't leave?

Yes. Well, it never crossed my mind to leave. It is strange, though—you're really just operating in this information vacuum. I had absolutely no way of getting in touch with any of you. So there was no point worrying about Matt.

And once you realised that everybody who could come in, had, what happened after that?

There was a certain amount of milling around at this point. Everyone was desperately waiting for news, trying to find out what was going on. I was with one of the paramedics who I knew and we were listening to his ambulance radio. And what we were hearing was that there was a really big problem at the CTV building. All these people were trapped, and they needed pain relief and assistance.

But Civil Defence had asked all medical people to stay at Latimer Square, because it was safest to care for people there—the idea being that the fire brigade would work at the scene, get the people out and bring them to Latimer Square or one of the other designated medical sites. I mean, this is established policy: you want to get the patient out of the dangerous location and bring them to a safe location where they can receive organised treatment. It's called the 'scoop and run', and we do it in lots of situations. Say I went to a car accident in Kaikōura—well, sometimes we have to treat the patient then and there, but for the most part we try to scoop them up and take them back to the hospital, where we can treat them better.

Anyway, listening to the radio it became increasingly clear that all the people there—the fire brigade and the paramedics— were saying, 'This is getting ugly.' They sounded desperate; you know, they needed help. The whole situation didn't fit our scoop and run algorithm, because all the people there were stuck and couldn't be moved.

So this guy and I were listening to this, saying, 'This sounds terrible.' And we didn't have much to do at Latimer Square at that stage—we had become sort of supernumerary. So he and I decided we would go and see what we could do at CTV. I mean, God knows why we thought this. We didn't have permission to go there, and in fact we knew the explicit instructions were for us to stay at Latimer Square. But rightly or wrongly we thought, well, it sounds like we could be more useful there. And so . . . we picked up a stretcher. I don't even think we discussed it much; we just sort of got going. We got a stretcher and went to one of the tents, and started grabbing some basic gear. Drugs and oxygen and I can't think what else . . . it was poorly organised, actually. We just grabbed whatever kit was readily available and we put it on the stretcher. I grabbed someone's hardhat which was lying on the grass. We put a blanket over all the stuff and then we trotted off up the road.

So you just walked there?

We ran, actually.

Did you, at that point, kind of recognise how surreal the whole thing was?

Ah . . . I think it did feel pretty crazy. I feel a bit embarrassed about it now, really. It was so blatantly not part of the plan. It just seemed like the right thing to do at the time, that's my only excuse.

You couldn't see the CTV building from Latimer Square, but it was close. So we were weaving our way up the rubble-strewn streets, jumping over it with the stretcher. It was very dusty, I can remember thinking how dusty it was. But then we rounded the corner and the CTV building came into view. And, honestly, that was a whole other moment of revelation.

The entire thing had collapsed, and what was left was this ginormous pile of rubble about three storeys high. But the lift shaft hadn't gone down, so that was towering up still at one end, and it was on fire. We could see flames and black smoke . . . and then all these people, swarming over the mess. There were helicopters flying over the rubble, diggers and cranes. It was overwhelming. It was so terrible . . . it really did look like a movie set, that's the only way I can describe it. It was noisy with drills and sirens and the choppers. The smoke and dust. All these high-vis jackets. Embarrassingly it reminded me of *Towering Inferno*, a disaster movie from the seventies. Anyway, it was grim.

So he and I ran up, not to the burning tower end, but the other. And pretty quickly people signalled to us to come over, so I think we must have been recognisable as doctors. He had his paramedic vest on, I had my PRIME vest. And we had the stretcher. We got waved up to this area that was maybe . . . halfway up the mound of rubble? But it was quite difficult to get up there. In the end we had to put down the stretcher, and we went up individually. It was like scrambling up the rock wall along the esplanade in Sumner, you know, big chunks of rock you had to climb up. As I was scrambling up I slipped over something, something slippery, and fell down onto my knee. And as I looked down I realised it was someone's smashed head.

And then you have that moment, I suppose, that terrible moment of looking around and seeing what's really there. And when I looked at the rubble, dotted all over the place were these sorts of clues—a vest here, or a jacket or a hat. Bits of stuff I initially thought had blown about over the rubble. But then I saw someone's arm, and it dawned on me that these were bodies. Real people. And I guess that's when I realised how truly, catastrophically bad it was. That was one of the worst moments—a reality check, really.

So with that thumping in my head, I got up to where this platform was and where this group of people had gathered.

How did everyone seem once you got up there?

Stressed, but also quite calm. Tired. Everybody was covered in dust, and streaks of sweat. And this was a group of ambulance and fire guys. They were standing around these two entrances, I suppose, where people had tunnelled—or started to tunnel—passages under the rocks, and had located some people. David Richards was up there—and he'd obviously been up there for a while, so he must have left Latimer Square at some stage too. He was saying to me, 'Okay, so they're bringing people out, it's slow but they're bringing them out.' And he stationed me at one of these tunnel entrances.

The initial task was to check people as they were pulled from the tunnels—essentially to see if they were dead or alive. If they were dead, then they were going to . . . stay there. And if they were alive then they were going to be scooted back to Latimer Square. So David said to me, 'You do that,' and then he went off to one of the other tunnels.

What do you mean by 'tunnels'?

They weren't so much tunnels as natural spaces that had formed when the building collapsed. And people had been trying to clear rubble out of those spaces so we could get into them. In the beginning it seemed like the building had fallen down like . . . a Jenga game, you know. There were little cracks, bigger cracks and sometimes no cracks. This was a seven-floor building, right. But the ends of the building had moved apart, and these huge floor slabs had all dropped on top of each other like a stack of plates. But where I was stationed there happened to be a beam—a big crossbeam, like a girder, so maybe . . . 300 mm deep? The floor had fallen across the beam and then cracked, and it had created a little triangular space you could creep in through. And these floors hadn't completely pancaked. Well, the bottom two did, actually— anyone between those floors was pretty seriously squashed. You could see the floor slabs, they must have been eight inches deep, and then there would be a gap of about six inches and then the next slab.

The floor we were at—well, the little space where you could crawl between the beam and the floor over top of it —was completely full of steel and rock and reinforcing rod . . . and furniture. The others had been working there for quite a while already, trying to move things and get people out. They'd brought out a few—some alive, some dead, obviously. What they were really doing was crawling into this tight space and trying to move the debris, either pushing it out with their legs or bringing it out in their arms. They were cutting their way in with hacksaws and stuff. It was an absolutely tiny space. So I would do a very rapid assessment of the people they brought out to see if they were dead or alive. If they were dead, there was an area off to the side on a flat bit of concrete where bodies were being put.

And this whole process was something that really came to haunt me afterwards, because it was surprisingly hard to tell. You know, normally if someone's died you can check his or her pulse—no pulse. You can listen to their heart with a stethoscope—no heartbeat. Check for reflexes; you can flick their eyelashes or whatever, see if their body reacts to it. And sometimes you can tell by looking at them, as well. If someone's ashen white or ice cold or stiff, then they're dead. But the problem in this situation was that everyone was completely covered in dust—they all looked like they had makeup on. It was incredibly noisy, so you couldn't hear anything like a heartbeat, and my own heart was pounding so much that all I could feel when I tried to take anyone's pulse was my own heart. I could have held a bit of wood and felt it thumping away.

Some people were clearly dead, but with others it was really hard to tell. Everyone was warm, because it was so hot in there. Underneath us was getting hotter and hotter from the fire. I think when you're in such a state of panic yourself, a really simple assessment like what colour are they, have they got a pulse, are they breathing—it all becomes so difficult. I'd hold my face really close to people, to see if they were breathing, you know. But if someone's using a jackhammer ten feet away from you . . . you can't tell anything. So I found that pretty stressful. I mean, mostly it was fine, but some points . . . it made me really upset. This was actually how I found out I had PTSD. I was at some stupid resuscitation conference a month later, and they were saying, 'Now we check the pulse! Now we check what colour the lips are!' I had a total meltdown. Started shouting. Told the guy he had no fucking clue about anything. And that's when someone said to me, 'Um, Chris, have you thought about taking any time off?'

Anyway, I remember at one point they brought out a woman who I thought was dead. And then I got into a panic because I suddenly thought maybe she wasn't, and so I kept saying to the guys, 'I want to go and check, I want to go and check.' I started getting anxious. And one of the paramedics who was there, another guy I knew, said to me, 'Chris. She's dead. Let it go.'

Was it shocking for you? All the death, I mean.

It's the nature of the job, so no, not really. I mean, that sounds kind of callous . . . and it's not that you don't care, or that you're not affected by it. You always wish you could have done it better, or more kindly. I was weirdly affected the other day reading in the paper about that girl who died in a car accident—you might have read it. She drove into somebody else's car, and the other driver got out to help her. So he'd actually been in the accident himself, but wasn't injured. And this nineteen-year-old girl was mortally injured, and he was trying to look after her before the ambulance arrived. It was clear to him that she was dying. So he gave her a kiss goodbye, and tried to think what her family would have wanted him to say to her . . . it's heartbreaking. It's such a moment, to be with someone when they're dying. So you wish you could have done that.

But in the brutality of the whole scene . . . you can't. You don't even think about it—this is all retrospective. You just have to get on with it. You don't cry or feel sad . . . everyone has such a desperate desire to help. You sort of just think, 'Right, I can't help her, but maybe I can help the next person.'

So this went on for a period of time too. But then there was a terrible disaster, because a woman was brought out who had been trapped for ages . . . a young woman, twenty-something. And she'd been squashed in this tunnel, essentially folded in half, her legs out straight and her body over them like a hairpin. Stuck like that for hours. She'd finally been brought out alive—to much jubilation. And she was in the category of being whizzed off to Latimer Square. Everyone who had helped her out was thrilled—laid her down on the stretcher, you know, 'Congratulations, you're fine, you've made it, you're going to be okay.' And she got taken down to the ambulance and whisked away. A short while after that, a message got relayed back up to us saying that she'd gone into cardiac arrest and died in the ambulance. The reason was that when your muscles are crushed for a long time with no blood supply, the cells break down and release potassium. And if you suddenly decompress someone—or, in her case, unfold her—those toxins are released into your blood system, and can affect your heart.

Oh, god.

It's so much easier in hindsight—if we could run it all over again we'd have all gone to a tutorial the day before about how best to deal with crush injuries. I mean, I don't think there was anything we could have done differently . . . But it was just such a devastatingly bad blow for us. We'd got this person who had been stuck for hours, and of course your natural instinct is to say, 'God, lay the poor girl down, put a blanket over her, give her some pain relief.'

So things felt desperate then. And I think that was what sent me into the tunnel—because all these other people were stuck, and we could hear them further in.

What was that like?

It was horrible. I mean, you knew they were alive and in pain, but you couldn't quite get to them. And now we were worried about people having the same problem as the girl who had just died. For some reason, which I've never quite understood, one of the ways you can try and prevent that from happening is by giving people Ventolin, like you do for asthma. Which seems a bit bizarre, but next minute we had all these boxes of nebulising masks arriving, like what you put on the face of someone with really bad asthma. And Ventolin. The idea was to try and run pipes of oxygen down into the little space we could get into, and to try and get masks on them and give them Ventolin.

So that became our next project. The nebuliser sets come in lengths of six or eight feet long, connected to bottles of oxygen. I said to one of the fire guys—because I was familiar with the whole nebulising set up—that I would go in and put the masks on people. David Richards was doing the same, I think. It became very MacGyver-ish, because you had all these tubes you had to tape together before trying to crawl into the tunnel to reach to all the people we could.

That was one of the first things that involved me in going into the tunnels. Oh, and of course people needed pain relief, so we were going in and jabbing them with morphine or whatever. A lot of them were foreign students who I think had been taking language classes in the building? It made it doubly horrible, because it was so frightening for them—you know, it was pitch black, dusty and we were coming at them with head torches and needles. Awful.

So you were actually crawling into the tunnel at this point?

Yeah, I was. David had said to me, 'Are you up for going in?' and I'd said yes. So I gathered whatever gear I needed, and went in. The poor fire guys had been doing relays in and out for so long—they were hot and exhausted, it was a difficult environment. I mean, calling it a tunnel is really a bit of misnomer—it was only just wide enough to fit one man's shoulders in, and you had to lie down on your belly, not on your hands and knees. You sort of had to shuffle, like a snake, with your arms out in front of you. You also couldn't turn around, because there wasn't enough room, it was so tight. So you had to be pulled out by your ankles if you wanted to get out.

In my recollection of the whole day, which I'm not sure is even true, the people were unbelievably quiet. Stoic, for the most part. They'd been trapped for hours. The guys behind me would be calling up, saying, 'Shuffle to the right, you can get to a little space up ahead,' and so I'd be shuffling along. And then in amongst the gloom and the rocks I'd suddenly realise I was seeing someone's upper body, or someone's head, and they'd be looking at me with great wide eyes.

What did you say to them?

Oh I don't know, really. I think I did my default, 'You'll be fine, it's going to be okay. We're going to help you.' Even in the knowledge that they might not understand me. I guess you're hoping that just the sound of someone talking helps.

Did they say anything back to you?

Some did, some didn't. Some were unconscious. The first person I came up to was actually dead. And I think then the next guy was trapped by the legs, but we managed to get him out.

It must have been such a nightmare trying to manoeuvre everybody.

It really was. And every time there was an aftershock, the plan was to pull everyone out. We didn't want the tunnel to collapse on us all. I was wearing all the wrong clothes—I only had a shirt on—so I got scraped along my stomach and arms. Often we were two or three people deep when we had to pull everyone out again.

And the building was on fire—it was very smoky, so it was quite difficult to breathe, and it was noticeably warm. They were dropping monsoon buckets over us—so to add another level of sensory confusion, you were completely soaked. But inside it was very hot, and we tried not to dwell on the fire. There was a certain amount of irony in taking a pipe pumping oxygen into a confined space where there was already a fire, but we didn't have another option.

Going in and out, in and out, with the Ventolin was painstakingly slow. There were two survivors who were the most memorable for me, who really stuck in my mind. One was this guy the firemen had already got to. He was facing directly away from us, and the only bit of him you could see was the soles of his shoes—you could see them because they were white. So he had these white sneakers on, and he was jiggling his feet and shouting. One of the reasons he was stuck was because someone was lying across the top of him, and they were dead, among other things. There was also an Apple computer—you know one of those old desktop ones, the distinctive apple-shaped ones. He had that jammed between his knees, between him and the roof. I don't know why it struck me so much but, you know, he would have been at his desk doing his work. We had to kind of prise the body off the top of him, and then the computer, and get them both out. Eventually we freed him up; we pulled him, and someone pulled us, and we all sort of slid out like a string of sausages. And this guy—he turned out be a twenty-year-old guy—he'd been stuck for hours with someone lying dead across his back. He got out, and we were saying, 'Are you okay? Are you okay?' But he just stood up and dusted himself off. We were all standing around him with our mouths open, waiting to see what he would do. And he just stood up, and went around and calmly thanked everybody in the ring. Gave us each a little bow. And then he sort of . . . just walked off! With someone helping him, I sincerely hope. And he was fine. It was very humbling, his thank you. It was amazing.

Are you okay? We can stop if you want.

No, no. It's okay.

The other person I remember—although this one was worse—was a woman who was caught by her foot. She'd been stuck for ages too, because about two-thirds of her foot was stuck between two enormous bits of concrete. We'd managed to clear the stuff around her, but she was seriously trapped by her foot. She was sort of on her side, I guess, with her foot nearest us and her body away from us. I think she'd already had some pain relief, and they'd tried to get her out by pulling her foot and trying to smash the concrete, trying to move it and so on. By this time it was late in the evening; it was pretty dark. And what had been happening, actually—in a kind of parallel story—was that underneath us was a pocket-space full of people who were all alive in this little room. We knew they were alive because they'd called their families on their mobiles, and the message had been relayed back to us. But we were taking a long time to get this girl above them out. We had people visiting us saying, 'Look, there's a group of eight people exactly underneath you, we know they're alive and they can hear noise above them.' There was a bit of debate growing about this, about how long it was taking us to rescue the few people above them, and how soon we should get in the big equipment and try to cut our way through to the room below. It was a pretty horrible predicament, and the fire was getting out of control at that point. So there was a lot of tension developing—we were too slow, there were more people underneath than above, and it was getting hotter. Everyone was telling us to hurry up, and we were saying, 'We can get her, we can get her.' We didn't want to give up on her.

So that was the driver of us thinking, right, we don't have enough time to fluff around anymore. If need be, we're going to have to amputate her foot in order to get her out. We were given, for this purpose, a kind of amputation kit, a terrible-looking array of equipment. There was a horrible big wooden tourniquet which I'd never even seen before; you could spin it around and it tightened up. And then we had a little surgical saw and some drugs, ketamine or whatever it was. The intention was to go in, knock her out, put the tourniquet on her leg and then cut off her foot.

Jesus.

Yeah, it was starting to feel pretty terrible. I felt awful. So we started to shuffle in again—we'd done it loads of times already but it was still quite an ordeal, clearing the space, getting your headgear on, trying to negotiate the supplies you were taking in with you. And whenever we went out to plan or get supplies, we always tried to send someone else in to do some comforting, so when we wanted to go back in we would then have to yell at them to shuffle out again and make room for us.

Could you tell her that you were going to amputate her foot?

Well no, not really. She was absolutely terrified. We crawled in and, up by her body, the space widened out a little so we were able to squish in shoulder to shoulder and talk about what we were going to do. It was difficult because she couldn't speak English. We tried to comfort her, but I don't think we were really helping. And she was absolutely petrified, because she knew something bad was about to happen. We had the saw. And we had to put this tourniquet on her leg, below her knee. That was a terrible moment, because she was screaming, 'No, no, no, no!' And we were saying, 'Please, we're trying to help, we're trying to get you out of here.' I was thinking, holy fuck, please can the drugs kick in so she doesn't have to be aware of what's about to happen.

Her foot was jammed up against the concrete, and we were trying to cut it off at the ankle. But, because of the angle, we couldn't actually move the saw in the space we had. So, with her still in a panic, we had to back out all over again and come up with a plan B. What we decided on was an oscillating saw, a kind of electric saw you use for cutting metal pipe. The blade of the saw moves, so we wouldn't need as much room. So we'd already had to abandon this poor woman, and then we were coming back in with the power cord and the oscillating saw. Even saying it now, I feel so terrible.

And we were both feeling pretty sick at this stage, this firefighter and I. Once we were back in, with the new saw, we had a moment where we both looked at each other, and I think it was him who said it: 'You're about one hundred kilos, I'm about one hundred kilos. What's the worse that can happen if we just pull her?'

I thought about. What's the worst that could happen? We'd leave half her foot behind. Best case scenario, we'd pull it out and maybe it would be broken, but it would still be attached to her leg. We really didn't want to cut off her foot.

So we went out again, and got a webbing belt from somewhere—like a strop that you'd use for tying stuff down.

Was the woman knocked out at this point?

No, she wasn't. She'd had some pain relief, but I was saving my knock-out stuff for the actual amputation. Because then you'd have to try and keep her breathing, you know—the whole thing is so incredibly sketchy. But I think I'd given her some morphine, because I felt so sorry for her.

So we went back in with this tie-down, effectively, and we wrapped it around her heel and ankle, which were both exposed. We both shuffled back about two feet to give ourselves some room, and basically said to her that we would pull until something happened. We absolutely heaved the tie-down. What happened was that her foot just popped out from between the concrete slabs, still attached to her leg. Admittedly it was squished, but it was still attached.

It was such a huge relief. But then of course I had the sick realisation that we almost didn't think of it—of just pulling the foot out, which seems like the most obvious thing in the world. But at the time it all seemed so massive, these slabs of concrete pressing on slabs of concrete. It shows how totally fucked up your thought patterns are in a situation like that.

I'm worried that I'm upsetting you, making you relive it all. We can stop.

It's all right. It's fine. It's just a bit emotionally battering, isn't it. She survived, you know. And sometime later I saw her and the fireman on TV together. She really did survive.

I had a bit of a breather after that. I think more people arrived, people better than me, really well trained intensive-care paramedics. The general consensus was we should all be swapped out, which was fine by me. And I had this rising anxiety that I didn't know where Matt was, and I still hadn't called home.

You must have been so exhausted.

I was. I was just feeling so weird. I walked back down to Latimer Square, which was quite surreal, really. When I got there I remember there was a bit of niggle—'you shouldn't have been up there' kind of thing. But I'd cut my face quite badly and needed stitches, so had to sort that out. I found myself in the triage tent 3.

It was about one in the morning, I think, and Latimer Square was under control. So I said to everybody that I needed to find my son. I was trying to get a ride there, to the school, but of course the whole city centre was on lockdown because everyone was worried about looting and things, so all the roads were closed. There was a much bigger police presence than there had been in the beginning. I wandered up to a policewoman and explained that I needed to find Matt, and asked her for a lift. She said yes, and I hopped into her car, and she basically went scooting off around the cordon and took me as close as we could get to the school. I said goodbye and then went off with some trepidation, really, because the area was so damaged. Eventually I turned up at the school.

The person I met said that everyone had already been picked up by their parents, but the kids who were left were in Flowers House, which is a building over the road owned by the school. And so I knocked on the door, and there was Matty. And a few other boys—I wasn't the only bad parent turning up late. It was a fantastic relief.

Did you let yourself feel begin to feel emotional about the whole day then, when you saw Matt?

No, I don't think so. It's hard to remember. You'd have to ask Matt what he thought when I turned up; in my recollection of it, I was still completely in adrenaline mode and was mainly preoccupied with what we were going to do next. We must have talked a little bit—I know Matt was feeling fairly traumatised. It had happened when he was walking to class under a long stone archway—you know, those old buildings around the arts centre, one of those. And they'd basically had to run for their lives with stuff falling down behind them as they ran, like an Indiana Jones movie. I think he'd found it bloody scary, all this masonry falling at your heels as you sprinted away.

But I still hadn't called home—I think all the phones were down. None of what had happened that day had really sunk in. I basically gathered up Matt and we got out of there fairly quickly. I don't think I was very sensitive to what he'd been through at that stage. But we needed to make a plan, and we pretty quickly started talking about our next move and not dwelling so much on what had happened. It was about two in the morning by the time we left—pitch black and eerily quiet. There were no traffic lights, no cars on the road. No lights on in the houses. An eerie scene, really.

I wasn't sure what to do next. We had no sense of how bad things were further north, whether the road to Kaikōura would be open. So in the end we thought we'd head out to Sumner, to the McGillivrays' [Piera and Jamie's]. That seemed like the safest and closest option, only half an hour across town. In hindsight, of course, going out to Sumner was a terrible idea, because trying to get across the city was hopeless. But we didn't know that, and I also made the critical mistake of trying to get there by going through Brighton and the eastern suburbs, rather than straight through the Ferry Road way. We didn't know it then, but the eastern suburbs were an absolute disaster zone. So anyway, we set off.

As we drove it all just seemed to get worse and worse. It was confusing in the dark—no streetlights, only the light of the car to see by. By the time we got to . . . Bromley, I guess it was, it was pretty full on. There was liquefaction everywhere, coming up out of the streets. In some places a murky water would be pumping out of the ground like a fire hydrant, and in other places it was beside us like a river, and would then drop off into these great cracks or holes in the ground where the road had moved. The water was sucked away like down a plughole.

We were crawling along in the car—it's a confusing area at the best of times, and we had no light other than our own headlights. I realised that we were on the wrong side of the Avon River. It's such a narrow river, really, and on a normal day there are about five different bridges in various places that you can use to get across it, which then carry on to Sumner. But every one we came across was either destroyed or blocked off. As well as that, I was starting to worry about the car falling into one of these giant cracks in the ground. We couldn't really see the road as we were driving, and I knew that if the car got stuck in a crack we'd be in real trouble.

Eventually we got onto one street that seemed completely swamped. In the car headlights we could only see water in front of us, and it seemed to be getting deeper. We figured it would be better if Matt got out and walked in front of the car, because if he fell in a hole he could swim out, whereas if the car got stuck we'd be well and truly stumped, you know. So Matt was walking ahead of me in the car headlights. The water was about thigh-deep on him, and we just kept moving along slowly. Eventually we came to a bridge that was still intact, but which had a big crack in the middle. And there was a car on the other side—we hadn't seen any other cars yet, and it seemed like this car was doing the same as us only in the opposite direction. I hopped out of our car and started walking across the bridge—it wasn't long, maybe about twenty metres. This guy in his car started doing the same, and we met in the middle where the big crack was. He told me that he was trying to head in the other direction, but that all of the bridges he'd passed so far had been out of action. It had been the same for us the other way. We tried to assess if we thought this one—our last option, really—would hold us while we drove across, and we jumped up and down a bit and eventually we decided that we'd give it a go, knowing that we would each stick around to help the other if one of us got stuck.

I think he went first, slowly, and he got across fine. I did the same, and then we waved at each other and continued on our way. Once we were across the Avon we could creep around to the estuary and ultimately the causeway—all of which were pretty flooded. There was destruction everywhere. I mean, unwittingly, we had just done a tour of all the worst parts of the city, but we had no way to know that at the time. And eventually we made it.

And was everyone awake, at the McGillivrays'?

It's hard to remember, it's all so blurry. It was about five in the morning at this point. I think quite a few people had gathered at their place—because it's on the hill, and I think there was a tsunami warning in Sumner. Matt and I just collapsed and went to bed. I still couldn't call home. Esther must have been horribly worried but, as I recall, I still couldn't get through. I don't think I spoke to her until the next morning.

And what happened the next day?

Well, the next day I wasn't sure what to do—should I go back to Latimer Square, the CTV building, Christchurch hospital, Kaikōura. I had no idea. I made a few calls to try and assess if I could still help at the CTV building—the phones were working again by then. When I'd left the night before we'd handed over to the better-equipped search and rescue people, and that's when I went across town to get Matt. The rescue had carried on through the night—the same stuff that I'd been doing in the tunnels. I'd imagined that, in the fullness of time, those people who had been trapped underneath us would have been rescued. But by the next morning all the CTV rescue teams had been pulled out, as it was deemed to dangerous to carry on there with the fire. And it was relayed to me—I'm not sure how—that the group in the room underneath us had never got out. They all died in the fire. It was—is—one of the most incomprehensible bits to me. That in our first-world country, with all these resources, and these rescuers . . . and these trapped people, who were alive and had called their families overseas . . . we just couldn't get them out. And that's the horrible reality of it. I'm not blaming anyone here; it was just impossible conditions. But it was appalling.

I also called you all, told you we were alive and okay. Rang the Christchurch hospital and they seemed under control—or had plenty of doctors, anyway. But I rang Kaikōura and it seemed that they were inundated with people who had fled Christchurch and were now gathered there in a bit of a panic. I thought I'd better get back up that way; I think I left that morning. That trip was also quite complicated, because there was a huge problem getting fuel. There was a sense of panic in the city, people desperately stockpiling water and petrol and general supplies. Lots of the garages were out of fuel and there were lines for miles. But eventually I untangled myself from all that and got on the road. I was back at work that day, really.

Did you ever have a chance to debrief, or talk to anyone about what you'd been through?

No, not really. I mean, in the days that followed I just hadn't got my head around any of it. When I look back, I think I probably handled it quite badly. I went straight back to work, feeling irritated by the arbitrary mundaneness of it all, although it was a busy time because we had all these people who'd fled Christchurch and had left their usual medication behind, and it was tricky trying to track down all their records. We had people coming in saying, 'I need my yellow pills!' And we were saying, 'What yellow pills?'

I didn't have much time away from work at all, and there wasn't any debrief. I just plodded on and found it all difficult and irritating. I should have got some help, or talked to someone about it. But it was confusing for people like me, who had wandered into the whole situation. Everyone who was part of a group—you know, the fire brigade, the ambulance people— they had a coordinated debrief. There were support systems in place making sure they were okay. For the rest of us who went into the whole thing solo, we were a bit lost afterwards. I never saw that firefighter again, the one who I'd been with in the tunnel . . . none of the people who I had shared this intense experience with. But at the time I thought I was fine. I truly thought I didn't need any help.

And were you fine, do you think?

No, I don't think I was. The tiredness, the irritability at work—they were warning signs. And then I went to that GP conference, which I already told you about. That was in March, so a month later. As part of the conference we had to do an Advanced Cardiac Life Support refresher course. This well-meaning trainer was speaking to us, perfectly reasonably, going over how you might assess and resuscitate someone. And I was furious and kept demanding, 'Have you ever done that in real life?' Just got overly wound up about it. It dawned on me afterwards how that wasn't a logical reaction. Someone then asked me, at the conference, if I'd ever talked to anyone about what I'd been through. And I realised that I hadn't.

So when did you?

Over the years I did talk to more people about it, in an informal way. But it would have been much better to have had some kind of structured debrief. The whole thing has prompted me to make sure we have more debriefs at work, whenever anything particularly tricky happens. For example, we once had a woman drown on the beach, and it ended up being a long resuscitation process that went wrong and had lots of complications, and the woman died. So afterwards I organised a big debrief with absolutely everybody who had been involved. It's so important, and I realise that more and more now. You need to be able to let off steam, and discuss and acknowledge what happened and how it went. Whatever it is—good, bad, frustrating, sad. You need to be able to talk about it.

What do you feel now when you think about the day of the earthquake?

I suppose . . . I mean, I do feel proud. Proud to have been a part of it, and to have made a material contribution. I feel a bit defensive about it, definitely. We did a good job in difficult circumstances, and a lot of people took personal risks to provide care. So I do feel proud. It's hard to remember . . . to reflect on how I felt in that moment. Because when you're there, doing it, you have to put your compassion to one side and process everything later. Thinking about it now, what has me in tears is actually that other guy, in the car accident, the way he was able to offer some comfort to that girl as she died. I wish I could have done the same—I wish I could have brought that level of compassion. But in a way, the whole day was just a bigger-scale version of what we do every day, and I have to tell myself that part of my job is not getting involved, at that level. You know, we had a resuscitation yesterday with a guy we all knew, and you have to stop yourself from getting caught up in it, have to stop yourself from thinking, 'But I know this guy, he can't die right in front of me!' You have to take your emotion out of it, and that's what's challenging, afterwards.

Last year I did talk to someone who was there on the day, and that was the now-retired Police Commissioner who tracked me down and eventually brought about this whole Bravery Medal thing. When the earthquake happened, ironically a lot of the key senior emergency management people were out of town for a meeting—I think it was literally an emergency response training meeting that they were at. And anyway, on the day this guy was the acting Police Commissioner; I think he stepped up and took on this huge, confronting role. He was in charge of the whole CTV scene. He was there all night, I think, and the next day had to make the call for everyone to stop trying to get people out. Horrible. I hadn't met him that day, but he was there. And he was aware, too, that we were there alongside the fire brigade and the paramedics and so on—he knew there were a few of us random people who weren't attached to an actual official response team and had come to the CTV building of our own accord.

He retired from work last year, and in his retirement he made a project of tracking down the previously unnamed people who had been at the CTV site with him on the day. People like David and me, who had just walked away afterwards and never talked to anyone about what had happened. And so he was asking around, trying to find out who was there, and at some point my name must have come up.

So he rang me up, five years later. I gathered it was a policeman on the other end and was frantically trying to think what I'd done wrong! But after we worked it out, it was amazing to talk to someone who had been there that day. We talked about the smell, the smoke, the very specific feeling of being inside a building that was hot, but you feel cold. It made me realise how much it would have helped me to have had that conversation earlier. It would still be good to have it now—I know David and I have both weirdly avoided it, even though it's been hard for him as well. He was really upset about the girl who came out alive, and then went into cardiac arrest in the ambulance.

Even six years later when I think about the whole day, it still feels confronting. I seem to get sadder as time goes on . . . I feel more grief. I didn't feel sad for years, really, afterwards. But now I wish I could have met with some of the people there and said thank you, for the times over the course of the day that they helped me. Like the paramedic who said, 'Let it go Chris, she's dead,' when I was losing the plot about the woman who I thought might still be alive. I don't know why I never tried to track him down, to say thank you. Maybe I still should.

*

Matt: We'd just finished class when the earthquake hit. We were down at Cranmer Block, which is separate from the main school, down Gloucester Street. We'd just had geography and, I'm not kidding, it was a lesson on earthquakes. Everyone was pretty interested because we'd had the September quake at that stage, so people sort of related to it more.

Anyway, class finished and we were walking back towards the school for lunch. To get there, you had to go down this alleyway between two buildings—eventually it opened out back at the carpark by the main school gates. And we had just walked into the carpark when it all started. I remember these parked cars bouncing around everywhere. Like, some of them would bounce towards us and some were thrown off in the other direction. We all grabbed each other around the shoulders and tried to stay upright—you couldn't have run anywhere. It was so violent, much worse than anything I'd ever felt before. And behind us in the alleyway all this brick and roof was crashing down. If any of us had still been in there we would have been smashed.

After the September quake, we'd got kind of used to the aftershocks, and we all knew that feeling of staying calm and waiting for something to stop. But this was crazy, like everything kept on shaking and getting worse. It was so noisy. Around us there were drains exploding, and water was pumping out onto the street. And then it seemed to stop for a minute, and we all started sprinting back towards the school. Heaps of other boys who had been around the grounds or in their [school boarding] houses started running over to the school as well. There was water in the streets, and rubble. It was pretty scary.

We were all meant to meet on the quad, but it was pretty frantic because the teachers were trying to work out who was and wasn't there. I knew Dad was in town—I tried to call him but the phones were down, and so I sent off a text. And then at some stage I got a text back saying, 'Yeah, Westfield is wild!'—meaning the Westfield Riccarton mall. And I was like, is he joking? Does he have no idea what's happening? I reckon I'll remember that forever, it seemed like such a funny thing to say at the time. From school we had a view of the city centre, and there was just this huge cloud of dust rising off it. We could see all the damage to the school, and it all felt pretty major. I remember laughing with some of the boys, like, 'You just enjoy your wild time at Westfield, Chris—I'm fine.'

And then there was a lot of waiting around. It was actually bloody scary, sitting on the quad and all the while there were these constant aftershocks, and we could see the buildings around us crashing down. There was this sort of stone archway over the doorway to my boarding house, and part of the roof fell off and smashed through it. We could see it all happening but we couldn't do anything about it, we just had to sit there and watch. At each aftershock you just wait and wait, hoping it isn't going to rev-up to the point that everything comes down. You sit there and hope it stops.

Anyway, parents started arriving and picking up their kids. And obviously, for the boarders, most of our parents were out of town, but there was a system where you could get signed out to a day boy's house. I thought about doing that so I could leave school, but I knew Dad was in town so I figured I'd wait for him. When he didn't turn up after a few hours I knew he'd be off helping somewhere. I knew he'd turn up eventually.

Some information was slowly getting back to us all about how bad things were. Like, people were talking about bodies and people being trapped, and smoke and dust was still pouring out of the city centre. I felt really bad that I couldn't get hold of Mum—I'd tried to text her but I hadn't heard anything back.

Then it started getting dark, and everyone who was left went over the road to the newest boarding house, which they figured was probably the safest. It was grim, to be honest—no power, so we were all just lying in the dark in the lounge, trying not to freak out at every aftershock. It was about ten of us by then, me and a few other boys waiting to be picked up. A couple of international students.

It was around midnight and I still hadn't heard from Dad. I was starting to regret not leaving with the one of the day boys. But we heard this banging on the door, and someone answered and then Dad was there. He looked crazy—he was absolutely covered in dust, and he had blood all over him and all these cuts and scrapes. His shirt had blood soaked into it. I wasn't totally surprised, because I knew he would have been doing something, but yeah—he did look pretty shocking.

He seemed calm, but also like he was in shock. I remember he gave me a hug or whatever, and then started asking all the teachers if anyone was hurt or if there was anything he could do—pretty typical. I was thinking, 'Yeah, or maybe you could treat yourself to a break and sit down for one second!' He seemed wired, but to be fair we all felt like that.

At that stage he must have said about being at the CTV building—he felt like he might need to go back there the following day, and so it affected what we decided to do that night. That was the only reason we didn't immediately drive back to Kaikōura, I'm pretty sure. But I have no idea why we decided to go out to Jamie and Piera's—it was such a bad idea to go to Sumner. There were so many places we could have gone in town, but I don't think we were thinking straight. We were just like, yeah, let's go.'

On the way out we talked about how bad it was, and again Dad mentioned the CTV building and that a lot of people had died. But I had no idea the full extent of what he'd been doing. We were fixed on trying to get out to Sumner, which was actually really difficult. Everywhere there were just these huge cracks in the road, and you could see cars half sticking out of them, or sometimes just the very boot of a car—the cracks were seriously deep, and with the water was rising up around the car it was impossible to see where they would be. So I hopped out and started wading through all this water in front of the car, feeling with my feet first.

The other thing I remember was that we were on the petrol light the whole time, and we'd probably been driving for an hour. So we were definitely aware of that and just wanted to get to Sumner. It's weird to think about it now, walking through all that water in the pitch dark, but at the time the only thing to do was to keep going. We didn't really talk much. It was scary, but we had to keep moving.

Eventually we made our way to Sumner, and got to the McGillivrays'. I can't really remember who was there. It was so late, or early, I guess, but you couldn't really sleep. Everyone was in the lounge, lying there, and these aftershocks would be happening the whole time. You can see Christchurch from their place—like, it looks out over the city—and when you went to look out, the city centre was just black. Like a big hole. And it was like that for years afterwards, a massive black hole where the city centre was, dark even when the rest of the city had lights on.

The next day Dad was talking about Kaikōura, and he seemed in a real hurry to get back there. The petrol thing was a nightmare because most garages were shut, and the ones that were open had these crazy lines everywhere. I actually don't know how the Landy got across town with the fuel we had— serious credit to the Landy for that. But finally we got some petrol and headed home.

Leaving town, I definitely had this guilty feeling, and so did Dad. You felt like you were abandoning everyone. I could Dad was pretty shaken up, but I don't think we talked about it in great depth.

It's so crazy now, to think about what he'd just been through when he arrived at the boarding house. I had no idea. I suppose my main feeling on the day was that there was no way he wouldn't be doing something, or helping someone, and I knew to wait for him. I knew he'd come and get me, in the end.

After

Christchurch was the backdrop to my childhood and then to my teenage years at boarding school, afternoons spent catching the bus to Northlands Mall for rice balls and window shopping at Glassons, our white shirts sticking to our underarms as we swayed along in the after-school mob. When we were old enough to go out in the weekends we'd head in to Sol Square with our fake IDs, bright-eyed from the RTDs we skulled in the botanical gardens. We would order lattes from Coffee Culture, drive to Wanaka or Maitai for New Years, and spend our weekends trawling through the musty racks of Toffs, the secondhand clothing warehouse. In my last year of boarding school, we would drag our duvets onto the lawn and lie around in our pyjamas on the grass, eating grapes and crackers and talking for hours, everything ending and beginning at the same time.

Christchurch doesn't feel like my place anymore. So many of the places I knew back then have changed, been lost and then rebuilt in a different way. But I still carry Christchurch around with me. It never feels defeated; the city only seems to rise and rise—sprawling murals painted on the sides of red-stickered, half-destroyed buildings, new cafés appearing in abandoned carparks. 'This is awesome,' my friend from

Wellington said when we visited Christchurch one weekend, walking through the new High Street. A whole community pushing their way through the cracks, like wildflowers.

Once, in City Gallery Wellington, I stumbled across an exhibition by the artist Julia Morison called *Meet Me on the Other Side*. It felt strange at first, eerie objects and structures salvaged and reformed, taken out of context and made new. In some of the works, grey blobs—now dried and hardened—had oozed through wire or empty spaces, dripping over edges and pooling in lumpy masses. Monochromatic paintings hung on the walls, vast and textured, made from spilled liquor and silt, replicating Morison's alcohol cabinet which had smashed in the Christchurch earthquake. Her studio had been in the red zone, and this series of sculptures found their roots in damaged objects, things abandoned and picked up again, transformed. Familiar items like plastic bags melded with silt from liquefaction had been suspended in cement and resin. The blobs were solid but somehow still in motion. 'What is this?' a little kid beside me asked. His dad replied, 'You know, I'm not really sure.' I think that's how we all felt, afterwards.

*

After the Christchurch earthquake in 2011, I didn't ask how Dad was feeling. In the days that followed we talked about it briefly; he said it had been a huge day and I didn't press him for details. I think Mum was mad at him, knowing that he'd been up all night rescuing people only to get back and become consumed by work again, not stopping to talk things over or ask how her experience had been, waiting to hear from him or Matt and fearing the worst.

I assumed, the same way I always had, that, because he was doctor and it was the nature of his job, he would be somehow be immune to the grief. I felt sure that any responsibility he may have felt would simply slide off his back, like water. I was stunned for Christchurch, for my old school, for my friends who lived there. I felt for Mum's sister, Lucy, and her husband Trevor, who had also moved to New Zealand and were now living in Christchurch with their three young children. I felt for the families who had lost members, for the businesses that had gone under, for the ruined cathedral, for people's sense of safety, which had been shattered. But I thought Dad, of all people, would be fine.

Abi

In 2014 I moved down to Dunedin. I was about to begin the last year of my degree, and I was in—not a rut, exactly—but a headspace where I knew I needed a change. Dunedin appealed because Finn and Matt were there, both studying at Otago. I applied to study by distance from Massey and was accepted; I could do my work from anywhere. It seemed like too good an opportunity to pass up: my last year of university in the same city as my brothers.

I moved in with two friends from school, and four other girls I didn't know. Seven of us, in one tall brick house with white windowframes on Constitution Street. It was like being back at boarding school, an effortless intimacy between us. When the sun was out we would climb up onto the roof and laze around on our towels, a rotation of friends stopping by to say hello. Compared with Wellington, Dunedin seemed so casual and easy. Everyone knew everyone, or at least knew someone who knew you. On Friday nights I would head up to parties at Finn's flat, Matt turning up later with a crowd of people, our friend groups merging the same way they had when we were kids.

Finn and Matt, and then later Rocky, all played rugby for Dunedin's Alhambra club, and I would drag my hangover down to the field to watch their Saturday games. I loved to cheer them on, the way they always did for me and my creative pursuits. Back at his flat, Finn had printed out some of my stories and taped them up in long lines of A4 paper on his bedroom walls.

My parents came down to watch the boys' games, heroically driving the eight hours between Kaikōura and Dunedin each weekend. They made the effort in part to support the boys, but also because of what the club meant to Rufus. Ruf has always loved rugby—a passion stoked by my other brothers and their friends, our wintery Saturdays dedicated to watching them play. When the boys played at high school he would be there every weekend, doing the haka with them from the sideline. When he turned up to one of Finn's early matches in Dunedin, Rufus was welcomed as a supporter, the coaches firing good-natured banter at him while he stood with them on the sideline. And as the years went by he became a regular fixture at the club, sitting on the bench with the rest of the team on gameday, invited back to the changing rooms and then to the club afterwards for beers and chips. They made him the water-boy, and he would sprint onto the field at halftime, mostly ignoring the water bottles, and join the team huddle, the boys looping their arms around him to include him. During the games you could hear him shouting from the sideline, echoing the coaches' instructions. Alhambra gifted Ruf supporters' gear and often mentioned him by name at their end-of-year dinners (which he was always invited to). At events they'd get him behind the bar in the clubrooms, where all the different teams got to know him. If he was ever in Dunedin midweek, he would go along to trainings, wrapped up against the bitter weather. Rufus being included in this way—and to this extent—was a huge deal for our family. If Dad was busy with work, Mum would do the drive alone, there and back each weekend, just so he could have his time feeling like one of them, wearing the same uniform as his brothers.

Rocky was still at school in Christchurch, on the brink of joining us. Sometimes he would come down for weekends, sleeping on our couches and floors. For Queen's Birthday Weekend, everyone came down to visit—Mum, Dad and Rufus driving down from Kaikōura, Rocky is his own separate car from Christchurch. We'd watched Finn and Matt's game that afternoon and taken a family photo, the two boys streaked with mud, stoked with their win. After, we went out with friends for a jubilant BYO dinner, then taxied to St Clair, where my parents had rented a house.

The same weekend, Aunty Lucy and Uncle Trevor were travelling with their two boys from Christchurch to Ohau, car loaded up with supplies for a few days away. Their twelve-year-old daughter Abi followed them later in the day, catching a ride down with some family friends with whom they'd planned to spend the weekend.

When Lucy and Trevor arrived in Ohau they received a call from the police, who informed them that their friends had been involved in a major car accident on their way down. Another driver had run a stop sign, and Abi, along with her school friend of the same age and her friend's mother, had died on impact.

When the phone rang, no one paid attention at first. I saw Dad ask whomever it was on the other end to repeat themselves, then he walked outside onto the deck. I watched his face through the glass doors.

Immediately after the news was relayed to us, my boyfriend told us all to get in the car, and that he would drive us. It was 10pm, and Christchurch was five hours away. I sat in the backseat, next to Rocky and Finn, watching the coast speed past us, the sea black and bottomless. Every so often, my boyfriend would catch my eye in the rearview mirror.

Although I hadn't been there at the time, he'd been at our house the year before when he'd got the news that his dad had died. Matt had driven him home to Christchurch, to be with his family. Sitting there, in the car, I felt overwhelmed by how circular it was, the way life just keeps on happening to you. We drove. No one said much. Mum cried for the entire duration of the trip and, beside me, Rocky held my hand.

In the week that followed, death washed over me anew. For days afterwards I sat around their house, the walls adorned with family photos that would now, always, be from a time before.

I thought about Christchurch, now three years gone, hundreds of families forced to carry on through their losses. I was surprised at how much I'd forgotten, how far away it felt. I watched Dad pace around my aunt's kitchen and wondered if he was thinking about it again, too.

We decided to bring Abi home from the hospital. We put her back in her bedroom—it looked like she was sleeping—and we sat with her and talked and played her music. When she was born, Mum and I had made a *Welcome home, Abi* sign which we'd waved above our heads when she was brought back from the hospital. It was still on the wall next to her, faded and a little watermarked from where it had rained that day.

On the day before her funeral, my brothers and were encouraged to say our last goodbyes to her before the coffin was closed. We filed down to her room, silent and dreading it, knowing that we were far too emotional to come up with the right words. The moment felt too huge to catch up with, storming ahead while we staggered, slow, behind.

In her bedroom, we sat around the coffin and no one spoke. It felt clear to me that none of us was going to be able to manage a word. An irrational panic set in that we would never leave this room, that the tension would never be broken, that the minutes would continue to crawl by while we struggled to speak. We were caught in the magnitude of forever; I could already feel myself looking back at this moment, wishing that we'd said it better, that in the last minute we'd done more.

Then, out of nowhere, Rufus stood up and recalled a prayer. It's one that Granny used to say to us when we were kids, for the vulnerable minutes before sleep and dreams.

God bless,
and Angels keep,
and guard you safely
while you sleep.

His words were a swift release from our silence. I was shocked he could even remember the prayer, let alone that he instinctively knew how much we needed it. We moved around him, holding his hands while he went on speaking for all of us. 'Abi,' he said simply, 'we love you. We will miss you.' Afterwards, outside the room, we blinked in the sudden light and we turned to thank Rufus, our little brother, who is so full of love, so ready to look after us.

Hard work

People always ask why none of us followed in my father's footsteps and became medical professionals. I had never been a likely candidate, scraping through science at school and chasing the arts at university. Every year it seemed I had about five different part-time jobs—nannying or hospo, or once, horrifically, a sales job in Auckland where I walked around door-knocking and being shouted at, writing short stories in my evenings at home.

After high school Finn became a raft guide, working a season in Nepal and then Rangitata. He once told me that when he looked at a river he could see everything: the hidden rocks, the push of certain currents, the route through shining out at him like a trail of lost coins. He studied adventure tourism at Otago, and when he was done he changed tack and got a job on the racing yacht *Leopard 3*, where he's been for the last two years, working twelve-hour days, long weeks away at sea. When he's gone I feel like I'm missing some crucial limb—I pick up the phone to call him and remember all over again. I imagine him on the night watch, loving it like Dad did, suspended somewhere between the sea and the sky.

We joked that no one knew what Matt actually did at uni. Finn and I would laugh at our big-hearted little brother, calling home with a hoarse voice from shouting over music at festivals or bars. He remains the most infectiously warm-hearted person I've ever met, at six feet tall and still with the same physically expressive personality he had as a kid. We call him the BFG, after Roald Dahl's character. Career-wise, my parents fretted for us all, but I remember Mum once saying that Matt was the one she worried about least; he just made people feel good, he would always find his way in life. Maybe it's unfair how much trust we place in him, simply for being kind and funny.

In his holidays Matt always tracks down farm work—he loves the landscapes, the hard physical work. He's finished uni now and gone travelling, calling home each time with new plans: van trips through Central America, an impossible amount of festivals. He ran out of money on the first leg, headed home and then to Australia to earn money working in the outback, driving tractors for the harvest. I thought he would be lonely out there in the brutal heat, the expansiveness. But he loved it, marvelling over the size of the machinery, the dead-straight dusty roads, the sheer, vast scale of everything.

Out of all of us, Rufus wants to be a doctor the most. His long-term passion for *Shortland Street* has equipped him with an impressive medical vocabulary, and he will often feign receiving phone calls as though he is a doctor on call. 'Rufus Henry, GP,' he'll say, picking up his phone at random during lunch. 'Right . . . incoming patient hit on the head by a rock . . .' (Rufus mispronounces some of his R's for W's, so in his low, gruff voice, it's 'hit on the head by a wok'.) 'Yes,' he'll say, 'send them to me, please. We are going to need a CT and some bloods.' When he hangs up, he always sighs with frustration. 'Work!' he mutters. 'They want to change the roster. I am on call tonight, sorry Esther.' He directs this last statement at my mother, mimicking Dad.

For a while it seemed like Rufus would never find a job

that fit. At first, life after high school had been hard for Mum, who stayed home each day to look after him, feeling guilty that there wasn't enough for him to do. We knew that if he lived in a city he would have access to better disability services—a truth that frustrated my parents, who felt it unfair that living rurally put him at such a disadvantage. He had a variety of shifts for one day a week at various places around Kaikōura—a café, the recycling centre. But nothing paid, and nothing was constant enough to allow him to set up his own independent life. My parents worried endlessly about what his future would look like, whether they were being selfish staying in Kaikōura, where there were no disabled groups or classes, no friends who shared his needs and challenges. When we were away—at school, uni or work elsewhere—Ruf was lonely. As much as my mother tried to fill in his days, she recognised he was a young man now; he craved independence, he didn't want to spend every day with his parents, at home. I've had many conversations with Rufus where he's begged me to take him to university. We've always been frank with him in these conversations, explaining that he's different, that although we know it's unfair, he just can't do the same things we can. There were times, especially during my last year in Dunedin, when Matt, Finn and I would be out in a bar somewhere, and we'd talk about what it would be like if Ruf had been born like the rest of us, if he'd never had Down's. He might have been there with us. In the summer of 2016, all of us but Rufus went to a festival together for New Years, Rocky joining us for the first time, finally eighteen. Ruf sat in the car on the day we left, refusing to get out because he so wanted to come. Again, we were frank with him, explaining that he wouldn't like the crowds, the drunkenness, the late nights. It was true—he wouldn't have liked it—but it didn't take away the guilt we all felt.

Friends are always surprised when they meet Rufus. 'Sup, boys,' he'll say, adopting my brothers' jocular speech, slapping hands in the same way he sees other guys his age do. He has such a strong, natural sense of self. You hear people comment on the many positive traits associated with Down syndrome— as in, 'Oh, they are so loving, they are so open, they are the sweetest kids.' And while in some ways that's true, Rufus is so much more complex than that, getting angry or upset, feeling the unfairness of his situation and rising to the challenge anyway. In early 2017, an engineering company called Dunlea Products reached out to Rufus and offered him some work. A real job, nine to five, five days a week. Mum sent us a photo of him the morning of his first day, blue overalls and black boots, a grin from ear to ear.

For a while it seemed like Rocky might pursue medicine. He has the best head for science, and has always been organised and methodical. Coming after Rufus was tough for Rocky, forced to hold his own against a tide of older siblings. When he was little, he requested a safe for his birthday—he had hopes for a more sophisticated security system than shut doors, something that would finally prevent his older brothers from barging in and taking his things. He became something of a conman in his attempts to look after himself, slyly convincing us we didn't need some old toy and then selling it for a killing on Trade Me. He was quieter than the rest of us, more thoughtful, less likely to gush out whatever thought passed through his head. Like me, he's a reader, and we still sit up at night sometimes with our books. He's also so much like Dad: the photos of eighteen-year-old Chris could easily be nineteen-year-old Rocky, the exact same serious expression, concentrating. Mini-Chris, Mum calls him, when he motors around in our fishing boat, drives down the coast for another afternoon of free diving.

When he finished school, Rocky went overseas and joined

Finn on *Leopard 3*, the two of them working together for a year. They sent us photos of them sitting out on the deck of the boat as the sun set, or drinking beers on the beach in some small Spanish town. When Rocky returned, he went to study geography at Otago, playing in the Alhambra rugby team which first Finn and then Matt had been captain of.

Dad always joked, when people asked, that none of us wanted to be doctors because we'd watched him do it and decided it looked too much like hard work. This was supposed to be funny, but it was also true in a way that made me sad. It was a privilege to grow up with a parent who was passionate about their work, but we also witnessed his passion be repeatedly stamped out. When the rewarding moments came, he had neither the time nor the energy to acknowledge them.

Being a medical professional in a rural setting requires a different skill set from what's required in an urban centre. On a basic level, this is to do with geography—in Kaikōura, we are almost three hours from the nearest big hospital. In the case of a serious car accident, the local doctor needs to be able to provide emergency assistance until the patient can be flown or driven down to Christchurch. Geography also affects the ease with which care can be provided. If you're an isolated farmer, then obviously it's more difficult to get to the doctor's appointment; to the mammogram, or the smear test. It's expensive, and it's a day off the farm. Who's going to do the milking if you're not there? So, as Dad says all the time, health services need to be delivered differently.

There's also the matter of on-call work. If you're a GP in the city, there's an after-hours service funded, whereas in rural settings, one of the doctors who has been working during the day remains on call. To be on call you need to be prepared for anything to come through the door, so it requires doctors who have broad training and experience. And while students start off with broad training, if they then head down an urban medical pathway for five years it can seem daunting coming back to rural medicine. Dad's found that even an experienced GP coming to do a locum in Kaikōura can feel nervous, thinking something along the lines of, 'Oh god, I haven't been to a car accident since I was a student, how will I cope with that?'

In the beginning, Dad loved the scope of work. His days would be so full and varied: he might be delivering a baby in the morning, racing off to an accident in the afternoon, taking a sexual health clinic at the high school and in between being presented with unusual farm accidents or medical dramas. It was exciting. He didn't mind getting up throughout the night, driving into the countryside to see sick children, attend to people's panic attacks, mediate drunken fights.

However, even in his early years working in Kaikōura, it was clear that recruiting young doctors who could then develop the required skill set was going to be a struggle. Talking to Dad about this, he explains to me how the health of a community is tied up with the rural economy. If you have a vibrant town, with good employment, medical facilities, schools, community spaces, internet and a thriving shopping centre, then everyone does better. People are attracted to work and live there, and that then attracts a better range of services. But if you have a town that's economically struggling—the meatworks have closed, there's high levels of unemployment and alcohol and drug abuse—then all the services basically stop coming. The schools suffer, people don't want to live there, and it's even more difficult to recruit to that area. So it becomes impossible to separate the health of a community from the economic wellness of that community.

For many economically struggling rural communities, medical recruitment is an issue. But as well as that, there seems to be a general (and, Dad would say, correct) perception among medical students that rural health services are inadequately funded. Young doctors, finally coming out the other side of their rigorous studies, most with massive student loans, would generally look at their options and perceive a specialist career in a city centre as being better-paid, with fewer or no nights on call, in a location that offers a better lifestyle.

What this looks like now in New Zealand is a depleted rural health workforce that is running out of energy. The average age of rural doctors is mid-fifties—my Dad's age—and the average age of rural nurses is only a couple of years behind. Aside from the fact that there aren't enough experienced people to take the pressure off rural doctors in an everyday sense, it also means that many rural medical professionals are worried about what will happen in the next five or ten years, when our current GPs will want to retire and there's no one to fill the space they leave behind.

There were a few years in Kaikōura when the practice had lost one of their doctors, and Dad's workload seemed to grow from already huge to overwhelming. He worked days from first thing in the morning till about 3 am the next day, not having stopped to eat or rest. Exercise was impossible; holidays seemed impossible. Days off were plagued by paperwork, and the stories he used to tell us about fascinating days at the office became less and less frequent, rare moments at home instead taken up either by sleep or a kind of manic attempt to help Mum maintain our cranky Clarence farmhouse—fences needed repairing, a water system needed fixing, gutters and lawns needed attending to.

We felt increasingly worried about him, arriving home starving at the end of each day, staggering off in the middle of the night for his on-call with a kind of heavy, bone-deep tiredness that made us worry for his driving, let alone the patients he was seeing. In the supermarket, local people would stop him to chat and ask questions, taking off their shoes to show him healed cuts and bunions, demonstrating limps or passing him their unwell babies. Seeing people talk to him stopped feeling nice, and started feeling relentless. *Stop!* I felt like shouting at them. *Let him be.*

It was a relief to have Clarence. Dad always loved that drive—thirty minutes along the highway and then fifteen minutes up into the valley—the rugged coastline, the mountains, the choppy, green-grey sea. The drive was a chance to wind down, usually in total silence, work a long way away by the time he walked through the door. He always seemed relieved when he arrived home, tossing his phone into our little office room off the kitchen, sinking down into a chair.

'Who can I talk to about all this?' Mum would demand, wanting a number she could call, a manager, someone who would listen to her fears for Dad's safety, his patients' safety. But there didn't seem to be anyone. The problem was too complex, there was no easy fix that didn't involve Dad retiring in his early fifties, leaving us with no income and kids still at home. Discussions about what to do fuelled our dinner conversations, Dad practically unconscious in another room, sprawled across the sofa deep in sleep. No matter how much we talked, we ran into dead ends, an endlessly complicated web of variables that left us with no room to move. 'He just needs to leave,' one of us would conclude, with outraged finality. But he couldn't, and so he didn't. We felt guilty, and then he felt guilty, and so it went on in the blur of weeks and months. Rufus finished high school, in 2013 I celebrated my twenty-first and then so did Finn, so did Matt. It got worse and then better, and then worse again, the odd weekend off appearing at the last minute like a cheap bandaid, stuck on hopefully as we cheered him on. In the end, we ignored the problem like unpaid bills with faraway deadlines. It was the kind of worry that would arrive sharply in the middle of the night, but in the bright light of morning seemed dulled again, easier not to think about.

Election 2017

I have started taking my laptop to cafés in Wellington, just to get out of the house and out of my own head. I've never done it before; it always seemed cliché, and kind of expensive because you have to buy stuff for them to let you sit there. But I park up in a back corner, order a tea and enjoy myself, watching people come and go while I work. Sometimes I look up from my computer and drop into conversations—once, a cool-looking couple have a loud discussion about a friend of mine, a musician. Isn't he wonderful, they agree, and I hide a smile.

Everyone's talking about the election, will Labour get in or won't they. I find myself having heated, unnecessary arguments with friends when we go out to parties. Twice my roommate and I get home from a night out and burst into tears. We try to follow it all, the frantic back and forth, our faces lit up by our phones in the dark of our room. The kids I nanny ask endless questions, a tonic to the angry things I'm reading on Twitter. 'Does Bill English like motorcycles?' they want to know, one drizzly afternoon when we are walking home from school. 'Motorcycles are *bad* for the environment.' I do my best to answer these questions fairly, but the kids unfailingly pick up on every word I say. 'It doesn't matter,' the boy says conclusively when we reach the house, 'it is not my turn to vote.' He looks at me. 'I am only five.'

*

In early September 2017 I fly down to Dunedin to meet my parents. Dad has been asked to make a speech at the annual lunch for the Life Members of the Otago Rugby Football Union. Each year the lunch is held at a different club, and this time it's at Alhambra. They invited our family along too, which probably isn't the usual protocol, but it's nice to be going. Rufus can't wait; he's pacing impatiently around the motel room, acting like he organised the whole lunch himself, telling us to hurry up and checking his watch obsessively. He's clearly angling to ditch us for his beloved Alhambra coaches the minute we arrive, because he keeps casually asking, 'So, where are you guys sitting?'

Dad is nervous, also pacing. He's been asked to talk about his experiences as a doctor, something to entertain the hundred-odd old boys in attendance. We can see them all from our window starting to arrive, crossing over the field towards the clubroom. They are grey-haired, most of them, still wearing their club blazers and ties. I think Dad actually feels a bit intimidated—all these old-school, hardcase, Southland rugby blokes.

We are seated at the Alhambra table. The guests are beaming around at each other, old friends, standing up to shout out to familiar faces on other tables. It's such a New Zealand scene, the tables lined with plastic jugs of beer, cubed cheese on the cheeseboards, sliced oranges. As the lunch begins all the Life Members stand up. They're asked to sit down in order of age until the oldest man is left standing—he's ninety-two, and everyone cheers for him; he grins from ear to ear as he sinks back into his seat. Rocky is with us, the only Henry left in Dunedin now, and the coaches come over to dish out banter, giving Dad a hard time for being nervous. 'He'll be fine,' they say to me, clapping Dad on the shoulder. 'He's a top bloke, your old man!'

When he stands up to make his speech, I am surprised to hear him talk about the CTV building—he's never mentioned it in public like this before. He talks about his role there, crawling in and out of the tunnels, a three-man-deep chain of doctors and firefighters clutching each other by the ankles, yanked out at every aftershock. He starts to talk about his feelings afterwards, the stuff that he never dealt with. Bravery wasn't so much required at the time, he says—that was instinct. Bravery was required later, in the years that followed, trying to make sense of what happened there, trying to admit to himself and others that he was struggling. The room, which until then had been noisy with people dashing back and forth between tables and the bar, is completely silent. Towards the end of his speech, Dad talks about the role of rugby clubs. He's seen it in his own sons, he says, the importance of having a place to belong. He says that if he could give any message, it would be that in order to look after our boys, we have to do our best to demonstrate to them that bravery comes in many forms; we need to lead by example, face the hard topics and allow ourselves to be vulnerable. When he finishes, all the men in the room leap to their feet, a standing ovation. A couple of them look teary, furiously clapping. I catch eyes with Mum, stunned. We look around the room in amazement—they are so ready for this stuff, all of these staunch, rugby guys. 'Thanks, mate,' they say later on, coming up to approach Dad. 'Really. Thank you.'

*

Later that same month, the election happens. I go around to my old flat to watch it, and we make a big dinner and sit in the tiny lounge, friends perched on the edges of couches, sitting on cushions on the floor. National leads, Labour is behind, and there's no definitive answer on who's in because we have to wait and see who Winston Peters sides with. We all feel deflated—there had been so much build-up for such a vague, washy result. We wander down to Cuba Street. Laundry bar is packed. It feels like a wake, so much emotional tension suddenly released, regardless of who you were rooting for. I think about the kids again, our conversations walking home from school. They'd often ask me why people voted for different parties. (This was after we'd got to the bottom of that confusing word, 'party'.) I'd told them it's because different things matter to different people, and so we vote according to the things we care about. 'What do you care about?' they asked, heads tipped back to look up at me. 'Um,' I said, 'finding better ways for people to look after each other. What do you care about?'

The eight-year-old's brow furrowed in concentration. 'My netball team. And no more motorcycles.'

On the way home from the bar, my friend finds an abandoned wooden pallet that someone's chucked out on the street. 'Yes!' she shouts, elated—she's been trying to find one to turn into a garden bed. It takes about six of us to carry it, but we run it back up to Tasman Street. It's a good end to the night—a random, happy thing.

She spends the following day transforming it, planting veges and flowers. We drive into town to pick up more soil, attempt to carry the dead-weight bags of it up our stairs. They seem to split wherever we touch them, and soon we are spilling little Hansel and Gretel trails behind us as we stagger onwards. Halfway up we catch each other's eyes, breathless and panic-stricken. 'Don't look at me,' my friend gasps. 'I think I'm going to start laughing.'

Kaikōura, 14 November 2016

It's strange when earthquakes start to seem normal, even inevitable, just random but regular things that happen, like storms. A little jolt—you look up and say, Oh! Earthquake! But then you move on again, back to work, back to whatever you're doing.

In the middle of the night, I woke up to find the house moving. Earthquake, I thought, watching the walls ripple, my heart drumming. I staggered out of bed, every step loaded with the unsettling sensation of missing a stair, my feet searching for the ground as it rolled away from me. I could hear my flatmates screaming upstairs. 'Should I stand in the doorway?' I shouted up to them, my body bent and clutching the walls as the floor kept moving.

When it stopped, all I wanted was to sleep, an illogical panic taking over that I would be exhausted for work the next day. When I woke again at 6 am, I had missed calls and messages from friends wanting to know if my family were okay. Shortly after, a message from my boss: work cancelled, the CBD closed down.

The quake had struck two minutes after midnight, with a magnitude of 7.8. As I flicked through news headlines, the word 'Clarence' stood out. I stared at the red rippling dot on the photos in the news, hovering—alien—over my hometown. It was raining outside, the sky grey and overcast. I sat on the stairs with the girls, shivering. None of us had work, and outside the street was eerily quiet, the city on hold. We were uneasy, jumpy, unsure what to do with ourselves. The phone lines were down in Kaikōura so I couldn't call anyone. We hugged each other, turned the heater on—a treat—and made pancakes, dark thick coffee somehow shocking us back to life.

I thought of Mum in Clarence. I didn't even know who was with her—maybe my cousin Hebe, visiting from England for the summer. Who else? I had talked to her the day before but it was so hard to keep track of the boys. Maybe Finn was home? Rufus? I couldn't remember. Dad had been on call, staying in Kaikōura the previous night—I knew that because I'd talked to him on the phone. We often joked that Clarence would be the best place to hide out during an apocalypse, stocked with months of food, a chest freezer of homekill meat, a lifetime supply of firewood. I imagined them playing boardgames by candlelight, heating up water and cooking toast on the Aga. I wasn't worried, but I would have liked to hear their voices.

Reports started coming in about the Clarence River. Residents should be warned; a wall of water coming, a dam burst somewhere upstream. A new wave of messages flooded my inbox, but there was nothing I could do, still no way to get in touch with anyone at home. I sat on my bed feeling helpless, dialling Dad's number over and over, his familiar answerphone message crackling back at me.

Sometime in the afternoon I saw him on the news. He was wearing high-vis and looked exhausted. He was being interviewed, talking about the two fatalities he'd been dealing with over the course of the night, the emergency procedures set up by the hospital, the vulnerable rural people they were still trying to reach. He asked residents to conserve water, to sanitise their hands, to sit tight because updates were coming. He was kind and reassuring and eloquent. I felt tears smarting my eyes. It seemed profoundly unfair that he was speaking to the nation but had yet to speak to me. It also seemed clear that the situation was much worse than I had imagined. I rang Aunty Lucy in Christchurch, who had already called to say she had Matt, Rocky and Rufus with her. We cried down the phone, frightened by how fragile everything seemed, another reminder that nothing was sacred, that everything was up for grabs—your child, your home, the ground under your feet.

Around five o'clock my phone rang, a picture of Dad fishing flashing up on my screen. I was surprised at the panic in his voice, a dramatic contrast to the man I'd seen on the news. 'It's not good,' he said. 'It's really bad.' He had been to visit Clarence and had seen Mum, momentarily diverting a MedEvac helicopter that had been checking on rural families. He'd been there for five minutes before he had to head off again, and I gathered their meeting—and his subsequent leaving— had been awful. 'She's distraught,' he told me. 'Everything she loves is broken.'

I was reeling. But Dad was still talking, telling me that our bridge over the river—the most solid and steadfast thing—was completely gone. I asked if he meant cracked, perhaps? Unable to be driven over? 'No,' he said. 'Gone.'

He told me to fly to Christchurch to be with the boys. 'This is big for us,' he said. 'Get there and I'll call you when I can.'

My flatmates drove me to the airport. It was pouring now, the rain humming all around us. I hugged them goodbye, our cheeks pink in the bitter cold wind. On the plane I pressed my head against the window and thought about home: winding up the road, the white limestone gravel, the intense green of the hills. Our house was always freezing or too hot, an archaic heating system fuelled by woodfire. It was a full-up place, dense in detail, with mismatched furniture, heavy wooden tables and fairy lights, a red Dunhill lamp, block-mounted maps hanging on the walls. Old photographs, shelves of books, pots and pans hanging from a rail above the sink. Home things, collected things, worn-down things. Loved things.

That night in Christchurch I slept in Abi's bed, feeling comforted by her pink possessions, her polaroids and fairy lights. She had hated the Christchurch earthquake, but I wished she were here this time around, her giddy laugh and the tight embrace of her skinny arms. I looked at her clothes hanging in her wardrobe, thought about the yellow dress she'd worn to her last party in Clarence. Mum would be up there now, in our house. All her things broken, no power and no knowing when she'd be able to get out. I wondered where she'd be sleeping—maybe they would sleep outside, so they felt safer? I was relieved that Rufus had been in Christchurch that weekend with Matt and Rocky. It seemed impossibly lucky that Finn was there with Mum instead of him. When I'd landed in Christchurch earlier that day, Rocky had hugged me, held my hand. He wanted to sit beside me all the time. How easily we could feel like little kids again, how much we needed our parents.

It was two days before Mum, Finn and Hebe were airlifted out of Clarence, all road access destroyed. At the airport we kind of fell into each other. We felt lucky, because we were all alive, but beyond that concrete fact everything seemed precarious, a map we didn't know how to read.

People used to ask me what Mum did for work—it's a lot of time, otherwise, to spend up in Clarence, tucked away in the folds of the hills. I'd explain that she looked after Rufus, who, despite being independent in so many ways, will never be able to drive and still requires a lot of help. 'But doesn't she get lonely sometimes?' my friends would ask, and I would think of the slow unfurling that had taken place within her since we moved there, an opening and a settling, a creativity given space to expand. In the years since my parents' separation, my mother had become sensitive and defensive, the wrong words or even just flippancy would have her retreating into herself, hurt and closed off again. In Clarence, she cupped soil in her hands and started to grow, claiming back a quiet confidence in the slowness of building and gardening and painting walls. To suddenly have such a clear, tangible answer to that question— *what do you do*—even if nobody asked her, changed her. Because the answer was obvious now: she had transformed a place. She had done it mostly alone, and it was hers, and it was beautiful.

On the drive back from the airport, I tried not to think about what it meant to lose something that you felt validated years of your life, the thing that gave you your sense of purpose. We knew we weren't going back there, not then, anyway; the roads were closed and the bridge was gone. Back at Lucy's house in Sumner, we tried to piece a patchwork plan together. Information came through, jumbled and scrappy, and we clutched onto it, going over and over the same bits of news. Friends came round to visit and we talked about Christchurch, six years on and still so many families left in limbo, houses waiting for repair. Lucy talked about Abi—how, in many ways, the immediate aftermath was a good time for them, all the family together, all routine stopping to make way for tragedy. Then how, as the weeks and months went on, life forced you to return to something resembling normal. That, it was clear, was the hard part.

When Dad came down to meet us, he told us how he'd been thrown into the role of rescuer once again, awake all night, tending injuries and fragile emotions, crawling under a building to pull an elderly woman to safety. He had stitches down his arm from where he'd cut himself on glass—the newspapers declared him a hero. To me he seemed pale and exhausted, thoroughly worn out and emotional. I was shocked to see him mourn the house so openly, to be so without hope of us ever returning there. I felt, even then, that surely we would go back. The road would be cleared, the bridge rebuilt, and everything would be fine in the end.

I put a call on Facebook asking if anyone had spare accommodation. A family we barely knew lent us their home in Christchurch, while they spent summer further up north.

Dad's friend and colleague Jo sent him a text following the earthquake, encouraging him to take time off and to look after himself. Dad had worked with Jo through the Rural Health Alliance, and often spoke of him to us with great admiration. Dad replied to Jo's message in a friendly way, and carried on— rushing between work and home, fielding media interviews and supporting those around him suffering emotional trauma, visiting local farmers on his days off, taking calls late at night while dinner stayed cold and untouched.

A few days later, Jo got in touch again.

Kia kaha Chris,
At risk of labouring the point, I didn't listen to the people around me and now I am a broken clinician. I can sense my clinical confidence returning slowly, but the sudden death of a young homeless man I saw a month ago in the new clinic we are setting up here has again destroyed my confidence.

I would not be in this position if I had listened and looked after myself better.

I know that in the midst of it when people said the same thing to me—and people did—we ALL have burnout stories—I thought at some level that person was weak and just couldn't handle it, that I was different, that I was OK, that I was doing enough to look after myself.

It is brilliant to be able to be heroic, to have the skills you have, to be the dedicated, delightful, funny and connected person you are, to be there for people in need, but you must look after yourself—the hard thing is to do this first and foremost.

We hear it every time we get on a plane—put your own oxygen mask on first, mate.

I am ashamed to say that while we read out this message many times over, marvelling at Jo's perceptiveness and genuine concern, we let the moment slip away. Dad was stunned by Jo's words, and referred to them often. There was a moment, then, where perhaps we could have pushed harder for him to recognise the road he was heading down—but it didn't happen. Dad carried on.

*

State Highway One—the main road running between Kaikōura and Blenheim—was devastated by the earthquake. Massive slips had meant total road closures north of Kaikōura. We could drive almost as far as the turnoff to Clarence Valley, but not quite. Two months later, we still hadn't been home.

When they'd been stuck up there, Mum, Finn and my cousin Hebe had done their best to clean up the house. Cupboards of food, stacks of plates and shelves of books had been thrown out from the walls, smashing over the floor in a sticky mess. The windows had popped out of their frames, and the pergola that Dad and Finn had built the previous summer—Mum carefully tending to the wisteria that had grown over it—had fallen down, beams of wood crashing onto pot plants and broken tiles.

Despite the basic cleanup that had already happened, going back there still felt daunting. On the long drive up in the furniture removal truck, we anticipated the pain of seeing our home unlived in and uncared for. To me, the house felt a like an abandoned family member, and our borrowed house in Christchurch like a strange betrayal. We imagined weeds forcing their way through the carefully tended plots of garden, the chest freezer of food that—without power—would have started to swell and rot. 'At least you cleaned away the broken stuff,' we said to Mum, a poor attempt at comforting, while privately we thought of the windows, and the rain and leaves that would have made their way inside.

It was clear that we would not be able to live in Clarence again for a long time. The bridge was still gone as if by magic, but a small back-country farm track allowed us to drop in to Clarence from behind, a longer route from the main road which involved mud and slips and a river crossing. To get to the farm track we needed to come from Blenheim, the top of the South Island—accessible to us then only via the West Coast, a detour that turned what would have been a three-hour trip into ten hours. The little farm track was usable in good weather, and its presence meant that the farmers who had stayed on their properties could make weekly trips to Blenheim for food and supplies. But it didn't help us, who needed a daily route out of Clarence to Kaikōura for Dad to get to work. That day, we drove in convoy, two cars and the truck, hoping to pack in as many possessions as we could, and knowing that a trip of this scale wasn't likely to happen again soon.

When we finally left Blenheim, heading down the coast towards Clarence, the land was devastated: torn in places where it had been forced upwards, the seabed risen metres and then harshly dried in the hot sun like a flat, salty cake. I was driving with Matt in the removal truck, and we sat in quiet grief as we took in the extent of what had happened here, passing family farms that had been literally ripped in half. Down towards the sea, railway tracks had been thrown sideways, curling like discarded, rust-coloured ribbons among the rock and grass.

We left the truck at the bottom of the valley, the road too small and winding to take it any further. I wanted to see the bridge, and so Mum, Dad, Finn and I drove one of the cars up Clarence Valley Road while Rocky and Matt joined some local farmers who had come to help us, commencing one of many furniture rescue trips up the farm track to the house with a tractor and trailer. Rufus was in his element, not remotely worried about the sadness of the day, more concerned about his reunion with Derek—one of the farmers—who loves to banter with him. Throughout the day Ruf rode shotgun in the tractor while we crawled up and down the little track, accepting more than his fair share of biscuits from Derek's wife Jane, who passed them slyly towards him while my parents' heads were turned.

Derek told us that he was keeping a little rowboat at the river where the bridge had been, which we could use to cross and get to the house that way. We agreed to meet the others at the house, in time to help them pack the first load of furniture into the trailer. The plan was to do trips all day, until the furniture removal van was full. It was going to be a long and difficult process, and we were relieved to be all together for it.

I stood at the edge of our road where the bridge had been. It was completely torn away, the road finishing in a rough tear, crumbling still as I scuffed it with my toes. Far across the river I could see the remains of where the bridge once met the bank on the other side, metal barriers curving down to meet the water like shining, wilting branches. The river itself had been disrupted, and now pooled, vast and murky, in a swollen lake. We tried to establish where it was that we used to sit—cold beers and stones hot under our backs—but it was too different now, changed, underwater. Our jump-rock had collapsed in a slip, and on the other side we could see the long tear across the earth where part of the land had been dramatically forced upwards, the road splitting and the river changing its course.

We piled into Derek's little rowboat in silence. In our arms we carried packing boxes, cleaning supplies, sandwiches.

Mosquitoes buzzed over the stagnant water, and in places we could see slabs of concrete from the collapsed bridge breaking through the surface of the water. It was so utterly changed from the fast-moving, clear blue river that we had so often swum in. I watched Mum's face as we crossed over, her mouth set, her chin cupped in her hands.

At the other side we scrambled up the bank, hauling ourselves up by gripping on to the ruined remains of the bridge, our shoes sodden from the muddy water. To our left, a scar swept across the earth like wake behind a boat, splitting the ground in two. It cut right across the paddock and out of sight, an angle that would have missed our house by barely anything. We walked in silence along the white limestone road, which had rippled and lifted so that we were now walking upwards on an incline. We didn't need to point out to each other what was different—it all was, a landscape that had shifted entirely. It was as though the ground had been picked up at the corners and billowed out like a duvet, new folds in place where it came to rest at our feet.

The house, when we walked up to it, was startlingly the same as it always had been. White weatherboard, the grassy path sloping down beside the house to the garden, walnuts crunching softly underfoot. The telltale signs of abandonment came into focus gradually: a wild cat hissing speedily away from us in fright, leaves blown over the doorstep. Inside, we walked from room to room, tracing with our fingertips ragged holes where the walls had ripped. Mum had left the house relatively immaculate, the same way she always had. I hugged her in the kitchen, which seemed so bare now, all the things that had been broken swept into the bins outside.

The others arrived not long afterwards. We started loading furniture into the trailer. Eight hours later, when we drove out for the last time, we were too tired to cry or even really comment. It all felt far from over; still the long route back to Christchurch and then the drive to Kaikōura ahead of us, then the unloading—into a rental house in Kaikōura, another temporary home while we waited for news.

When Abi died, we'd all felt the lingering trauma, afterwards. Two missed calls from nearly anyone would have my heart racing. 'It's okay,' my boyfriend would say, when I called him back in a panic. 'Everyone's fine. I was just calling because I'm in the supermarket. I didn't mean to make you worried.' In the car, Mum would gasp as we approached an intersection, her knuckles white as they gripped the steering wheel. When she told the boys to drive safely they would look her eye, never brushing her off as they used to. 'We will, Mum,' they would say seriously, often hugging her, all of them towering over her, apart from Rufus.

The earthquake was different—we had lost a home, not a person—but I could always feel it in the back of my mind. In Wellington I would catch myself looking at houses on the hill, wondering how each would fair in a sudden slip, imagining them sliding noiselessly down as I watched from a distance. I would sometimes wake from dreams convinced the bed was moving, crashing my hand over the bedside table to find the light. Mum had become jumpy at just about anything—loud noises, someone's foot accidentally rocking the table. Things that had never mattered before suddenly took on huge importance: a set of plates I didn't even think she liked rescued from storage in the garage, held aloft as the last, precious, unbroken ones.

We waited. Would we go back, or wouldn't we? Would the bridge be built again, or not? The process was slow, various chains of command needed to assess, reassess, discuss, approve, deny. In Christchurch, we were told, people were still waiting, and that was six years on. Six years of limbo, six years of life on hold. 'Don't talk about it,' Mum would say, 'it makes me too sad.'

Most of my sadness was for us as a family, but particularly

for my parents. All we could do was hang around, waiting to see exactly how bad it would be. Sometimes, though, when I was alone, I would feel a grief that was all my own. I would think about running, down the drive and past the mailbox, over the bridge, down the road which looped up into the valley. Underfoot first would be walnuts from the trees outside our house, then the cattle-stop, then grass and white limestone gravel. Frost, sometimes, or muddy puddles, cow shit. For a while the road ran flat and straight out in front of me, boundless hills on either side, layered against each other in shades of dusk, like a painting. I would run past fields of cows, who would get a fright and then canter alongside me. On my way back to the house I would stand on the bridge, watching the water rush past below, removing my headphones so I could take in the noise of it. All that time spent moving through the valley on foot; I ache with the feeling of being there.

A deep loss

In November, I ask Mum if she will speak to me about her experience of the earthquake—our earthquake, as we sometimes call it. I am home for a couple of weeks to write, having flown into Blenheim the day before, skittering unsteadily out of Wellington on the wings of another miniature Sounds Air plane.

The road is still closed between Blenheim and Kaikōura, but as Clarence residents we have what is called a 'convoy pass'—basically a season pass for the scheduled daily convoys that run through the construction. I've been on one of these convoys once before, passing through the dusty, seaside warzone swarming with workers in high-vis, the old road completely ripped up and replaced by the beginnings of a new one, looping its way around the giant slips. Yesterday we had wound down from Blenheim to meet up with the convoy. It was a journey in itself, the highway now dotted with stop–go's, long stretches of one-way traffic, half an hour of driving easily doubled by our crawling pace. When we arrived we were told the morning convoy had been cancelled, and so spent a long, frustrating day on the side of the road, waiting for it to open up again.

Today we have a funeral in Christchurch, and we are off again, this time driving the inland road, as the highway south of Kaikōura is closed for ongoing repairs. The inland road is the kind of drive that makes us despair of our earthquaked lives, winding and slow, punctuated with construction that halts the steady flow of traffic. It adds another hour onto the journey to Christchurch, and driving it gives you the frustrating sense of moving in just slightly the wrong direction.

Mum and I agree to pass the time with an interview. I am pleased she's keen to chat to me—it's not always easy for her to speak about her experience, knowing that, compared with others, our problems are fairly insignificant. For local farmers, the depth of loss continues to unfold, acres of paddocks vanished or swept up by the river, land that has been tended to for generations now destroyed, huge financial losses. Compared with them, so deeply familiar with the land, we are transient visitors in Clarence Valley, barely leaving a mark.

In the end, we talk for an hour. It's a conversation that is, again, void of any real planning on my part. When I talked to Dad about the Christchurch earthquake, I had been shocked by the emotions it brought up in him. I expected it more from my mother, but still it was hard for me to hear her grief, so unresolved, still so close to the surface.

Chessie: *It's weird, when I interviewed Dad about the Christchurch quake we were also driving from Kaikōura to Christchurch.*

Esther: I remember!

But he had my phone all rigged up with a bungee cord over the steering wheel so the phone was close to his face. Very dodgy.

Well, you won't have to worry about me rigging anything.

Yeah, rigging is not our forte. Anyway, I wanted to ask you about Clarence. I guess we should start from the beginning. Can you remember when you first found the house?

Yes, I do actually, because I was in the hairdressers'. I had my head back over the basin, having my hair washed, and the real estate agent—who knows us—was there as well. I wasn't even looking for a house at the time, but she came over to me, kind of leaned over the basin where I was lying, and said, 'Esther—I've got the perfect house for you!'

I hadn't really been up to Clarence before. I'd passed through on the way to Blenheim but it wasn't a place I ever really thought about. I drove up the very next morning—even though I wasn't really interested—and as soon as I got up there I completely fell in love with it, and that was that. Such a typical Chris and Esther move, although in this case it was just me.

Did you ever feel worried that it was so isolated?

I did, but that was the only way I could afford to buy a house, especially a house that was big enough for all our family. A proper house, with things that other people have, like enough bedrooms for everyone! Although actually it didn't quite have that. But it was big and roomy and had huge lawns.

I think also I had these slightly romantic ideas about this fairytale house, all tucked away—probably from reading *The Railway Children* when I was little. I wanted a house that would somehow capture everyone back again.

I remember when you first took me up there. I can vividly remember driving up the road.

I don't think anyone really loved it, did they! Matty said he was thinking, 'Oh god, where is she taking me . . .'

We all got over that feeling pretty quickly though.

It's awful how, as an adult, sometimes you have to know better than your children and think, 'You don't know it yet, but you will like this.' It was like an unlimited playground for the boys! They just didn't like that it was out of cellphone range, the losers!

Can you remember much from the night of the earthquake?

Well, the whole family had been at the Christchurch races on Saturday, and I'd stayed in town because one of the boys had taken Rufus to the pub afterwards with all their friends. Later on he got brought back to me, at the motel. But that night, Bella Eaton—so nice of her—invited him to her twenty-first birthday, which was a big lunch on the Sunday. So he wanted to stay for that, and Matty said he would take him so I didn't have to stay in town that night. Chris was on call, so he was staying in Kaikōura.

Finn, Hebe and I were all texting and saying how tired we were. And Finn said, 'Let's go back up to Clarence! We can get takeaways and watch movies, and it'll be amazing.' I was obviously thrilled with that idea, and so we all went back. We were so excited, the whole way back, feeling smug that we'd planned such a great hungover evening. No better place for that kind of thing than Clarence, as you know.

So we got back, did whatever we were planning to do—movies and takeaways—and then we went to bed, pretty early. And then I woke up to this violent shaking, and Hebe appearing through my door and saying, 'Esther! Esther!' She somehow climbed into the bed with me and we both just lay there. It went on for *such* a long time. The whole bed was jumping from side to side and the lights and the bedside tables were all crashing down. It was like nothing I'd ever felt.

Were you very scared? Did you ever think, 'This is it'?

I was too scared to think. I always end up being frozen to the spot if I'm scared; I can't think about anything. I don't wonder if I'm going to die, I just cannot move, I'm frozen with fear. And it seemed to go on forever. Later we found out it was something like two or three minutes. When it did eventually subside, we heard Finn coming down the corridor. He'd been in the sleep-out opposite the house, and he said he'd got up and stood there in the doorframe, unable to step outside because everything was shaking so much. But once it calmed down he crossed over to the house and made it down the corridor.

It was so lucky that it was a supermoon at the time, or whatever it's called, because you could actually see a little bit. I didn't have a torch by the bed—I mean, we have hundreds of candles—but there was so much glass everywhere. That big mirror above the fireplace had smashed, and there was so much glass in the kitchen. We could see because of the moonlight through the windows, and so we gingerly picked our way along the corridor with Finn leading the way, Hebe limping because the bedside table had fallen over her ankle, and we went through the kitchen and out the front door. I think for about ten minutes we just stood outside, not knowing what to do. And then the neighbours arrived.

Were you aware of how big the quake had been?

We were all saying things like, 'Surely that was a very big one.' But where was it big? Where was it worse? It never occurred to us that we were in the centre of it all. I was so worried about you, in Wellington, and the boys in Christchurch.

We were standing there, in the driveway, and there was so much noise—we could hear the landslides happening, the sound of dirt and land moving. It was eerily bright because of the supermoon. I don't quite know what the sequence of events was, at that stage, but we went over to the neighbours' and stood around there together. No one wanted to go into any of the houses, obviously, so we stood outside. It was a scary time—so much noise—and we kept frantically looking around and wondering where the landslide was coming from, worrying that it was above us. You could see great big dust clouds everywhere.

So we all stood by Gavin's fence. Everyone was shaken up. One of our neighbours had rushed out of the house in only a small nightie—you know, I just mean that as a way of explaining the absolute urgency and sense of disarray. It was really, properly scary. And it just went on and on and on being scary. No one knew what was going on—we all agreed it was big, but we didn't know where. Chris was in Kaikōura. I truly thought there would be much worse news somewhere else.

By the time it was light we decided to go back to the house and have a look. And then, well, I slightly forced Finn and Hebe—you know what I'm like—to try and clear it all up a bit. It really had to be done. You couldn't walk on any surface of the floor. The kitchen, especially—our cupboards were all so old; it wasn't like a modern kitchen where the cupboards are latched or weighted shut or whatever. They'd swung open and emptied their contents onto the floor. The floor was a huge treacle mess of glass and soy sauce and all kinds of random stuff. The fridge had completely emptied out.

There were still lots of aftershocks, but it was daylight and so it seemed easier to go into the house. And we thought, well, if it hasn't come down by now then it's probably all right. So we tried to clean up, just put it all into the wheelbarrow and dumped it in the bins outside.

Was that an emotional experience, throwing away so many broken things?

No, it was too messy to be emotional. The mess felt weirdly more upsetting than any broken individual items. They were just broken, and that was that. Nothing you could do about it. So we cleared up, which was very difficult without any water or power. We just chucked it all away, which at the time I vaguely knew was a bad idea because then you don't have proof for insurance. But they've been quite understanding.

We spent most of the day clearing. Finn was trying to board up the windows where they'd popped out of their frames, rope up doors and all that. It was good that we did do so much that day, because we couldn't get back for so long afterwards, although at the time we didn't know it would be like that. At some point we walked down to the river—which had actually become difficult, as the road was so destroyed. We were climbing over the rubble of the road, and when we got to the end the entire bridge had gone. Completely vanished. It was very shocking. It felt so enormous.

We also had two visits that day. And the first was from Richie McCaw! Which was honestly fantastic. We saw the helicopter land, and we all thought it would be Chris, so we ran down the field towards it. Some people got out, and they were talking to our neighbour, and there was another guy getting out, the pilot. Finn and I just looked at each other with these amazed grins—you know, we couldn't believe it was him, such an absolute hero in our family. Finn has looked up to him for years. Finn and I were trying to play it cool—we didn't want to make a fuss. And so we were chatting away to him. Basically he'd come up to check on people, I suppose, to act as a bit of a morale boost. Eventually I was like, 'I can't take this anymore: Hebe doesn't even know who this guy is!' You know, she's a London girl, so New Zealand rugby players are hardly her top priority. But seeing him was great. Such a random, uplifting, happy moment.

Hebe said to me later that she remembers thinking, well, this is obviously a good family friend of theirs, they're both so happy to see him!

Oh my god, maybe we weren't as cool as we thought! I said to her at the time, 'Hebe, do you know who this is?' And she said, 'No,' and Finn and I were laughing, like, 'Don't worry, we'll tell you later!'

He was only there for a little bit, but it was still such a great moment. Finn and I walked back up the hill, laughing like, 'Oh my god, I can't believe we just had Richie on our lawn!'

A short while later, we heard another helicopter, and that was Chris. I literally ran down the field crying, and he—I'm not joking—said, 'Hello Esther,' and then immediately turned to the neighbours and started checking up on them! I was thinking, are you kidding me?

To be fair, he'd had to divert the MedEvac helicopter that was supposed to be checking on rural families for injuries and whatnot, and so he did have to appear to be checking on people. And he could clearly see that I was fine because I was running and crying.

Ha—'She looks fine.'

Yeah, that's just normal Esther! I got to talk to him eventually, and I remember saying, 'Oh Chris, you honestly won't believe what's happened.' I said that everything was broken. He came and looked around the house, but so briefly, like he

225

spent about one minute in there. He was very distracted—and, you know, he'd been up all night saving people. I just remember him leaving, and me feeling so shocked at how he hadn't really paid any attention to us, our home—how he hadn't said anything at all. He was in his first-responder role, so I don't blame him. But it was hard not to feel upset that he was off giving everyone else so much attention at a time when I was feeling so vulnerable myself and needed my husband.

To this day I don't think he's ever taken on how it felt to be up there and go through it all. A couple of months ago he saw some pictures on my laptop that we'd taken of the immediate aftermath, and he couldn't get over how bad the kitchen looked with all the stuff everywhere. He was shocked by all the chaos. He had never shown any real interest in it before then—his role was so different in it all, we had totally different experiences. I think he understands now how traumatised I felt by it, and he knows that at the time he didn't have room to take that on. And I was fine, obviously. But I did feel, strongly, that we needed him and he wasn't available.

So eventually you were evacuated?

Well, our neighbour Shirley had some kind of satellite phone. I can barely understand what it was or how it works, but she was making daily trips up to the very top of the hill, where she could get signal, and messages were being relayed that eventually there would be an opportunity to be helicoptered out. It's hard to remember the timeframe. We had one more night of barely knowing anything, and having no real news. Finn and Hebe and I were too scared to sleep alone, so we slept on mattresses in the living room. I can remember lying there with my heart pounding, hoping each aftershock wouldn't be the next big one. And then the next morning Shirley went up the hill, came back down, and told us there was a helicopter coming in ten minutes for people who wanted to go.

A lot of people didn't want to go, did they? Because they couldn't leave their farms.

Yeah, exactly. Part of me wishes we could have stayed to sort the house out before we basically had to abandon it. But there was no way I could have done that. I was desperate to get to you all, and Chris. Needed to have words with him, clearly!

So we threw all our clothes into a bag. I had no idea what to take, and ended up with such a small assortment of things. Nothing, really. The helicopter turned up, and we left.

Did you feel, then, as you were leaving, the enormity of it all?

I did. I remember looking back down, as the helicopter took off, and just wondering when we would ever be back there again. Wondering if I'd ever go back.

Sorry—I know it's upsetting. Sorry, Mum.

It's okay. It does make me realise that it was a big moment. Anyway, it was a huge relief to be leaving. I'd been so on edge the whole time. We flew to Ward [a township north of Clarence], to what I guess was their community hall. It had been turned into a sort of emergency centre, and there were helicopters everywhere, emergency people—attending to the emergency!—and so on. The police there offered us a police car to take us to Blenheim, where we could get a flight to Christchurch. And Lucy had booked some flights for us, which was ideal. But I also really wanted to visit [our friend] Richard while we were in Blenheim, just to see a familiar face and to feel like there was still something normal that could happen in my life. I knew he'd be armed with wine, and would be so caring. But we had barely any time to spare, because the flights we'd booked were early that afternoon.

And so—I don't know if you'll be able to put this in the book, because it was pretty naughty of him, probably—but the policeman, who was a total legend, said to us, 'Don't worry, I'm going to get you there for a wine!' and he drove us *so* fast to Blenheim. It was so sweet. We got see Richard, had a quick wine and a catch up, and then he drove us to the airport, where we flew out to Christchurch and met up with all of you.

God, that was dreadful.

Yeah, it was. By the time I arrived it was really hitting me, how scared I'd been.

I remember us all being at the airport and feeling this massive grief, I guess.

Oh god, let's not even talk about it.

When did we next go back? I feel like it wasn't for about three months.

No, I think Chris went back a few weeks later in a helicopter and picked up some more things.

That's right. I remember us writing lists of what we wanted, but there was only room for about two bags in the helicopter so we had to choose really carefully.

For a while it felt like he was always flying around in helicopters. I think they were doing rural check-ups that way. But yes, I do remember him getting stuff for our long-planned family holiday up north. We nearly cancelled it, do you remember? It felt like such a ridiculous time to have a holiday. I actually emailed the lady with the bach to say I didn't think we could come anymore. But then we thought, why shouldn't we go? It was all booked and paid for, and it's not like we had anywhere else to stay! Why would you make your life even more miserable by not going on the holiday? And so the boys pulled off that amazing rescue of the boat trailer, because we needed the boat for the holiday.

What happened with the boat trailer? I can't remember that.

Well, the boat trailer was in Kaikōura, and so it was stuck because the roads either side were closed by slips at that point. Chris organised a rescue mission—he's quite matey with the helicopter guys because he does so much work with them. He was at work that day—I remember Rocky laughing and saying, 'Honestly, Mum, you should have seen him . . .' He was wearing all his proper work clothes. Basically he asked Rocky to drive from Christchurch as close as he could get to Kaikōura, and so Rocky drove up in the car and waited at the designated point. And Chris drove the boat—like, in the ocean—down the coast from Kaikōura to meet him. Rocky was waiting and waiting, and eventually he heard this *whip-whip-whip* of the helicopter noise overhead. He looked up and the helicopter was there with our boat trailer hanging underneath it. It's so old and heavy; you can imagine how outrageous it looked. So the helicopter swooped down next to Rocky and just dropped the trailer.

And Chris, who had arrived in the boat, was at that stage wading through the water dragging the boat behind him. But because the seabed had risen so much, it was all quite complicated. There was so much slime and stink and seaweed, and Chris was wading through it all in his work trousers. Eventually they got the boat onto the trailer, Rocky attached the trailer to the car and Chris hopped into the helicopter and flew back to work. It was definitely one of those 'Okay, well I guess this is our life now!' kind of moments.

Absolutely ridiculous.

Yup. But the holiday was back on. It was so good when we finally got there, because I had been unsure about going. I felt, at the time—and I still feel now—that it can't be okay to leave the house, and ignore that whole issue. I think that's partly what upsets me, that it's still up there looking abandoned, and no one else seems to think it's a problem that it looks so awful. I'd love to go back and take care of it, which a part of me knows is pointless . . . But the problem's not going away, you know, there's still so much work that needs to be done.

How significant is that feeling of abandoning the house to you?

It's huge. It's what Anne Marie [Mum's friend, who also lives just north of Kaikōura] and I always talk about. I don't know what, particularly, but there are so many little ramifications that continue to worry you. I felt so upset about leaving behind all my pot plants, and I still lie awake and think about how everything will be dying and getting overgrown. It's not the sort of house you can just leave, it requires so much maintenance. And I had spent so long tending to it all—the house, and the garden and the children. Now I constantly feel tripped up when I go to get certain things out of the cupboard or I remember, oh, that was smashed too. Or I remember I've lost something that belonged to my mum—I didn't have many of her things, and they've all been smashed. That really upsets me. Anne Marie was exactly the same, you know, like, 'We can't replace the things, because they were precious because of the memories attached to them.' They were things that we'd gathered over years, gifts people have given us that we'd treasured, like the vase you gave me.

Do you feel like the quake has affected you long-term? Do you feel any lingering trauma from it?

Definitely. I'm so jumpy. Chris is always saying how jumpy I am—anything will set me off, really, like a noise or a shake. The hairdresser said to me that I'd lost a lot of hair. Which hardly matters, because I have such thick hair, but I think it was something she'd noticed with a lot the women around town. I am quite traumatised by the whole thing, really. And emotionally . . . I feel very fragile. It feels like I'm operating on such a thin veneer, like one small thing goes wrong and everything comes crashing down. Life still feels difficult all the time.

Well, yesterday and today are perfect examples of that.

Yes, exactly! Just that daily niggle of everything being harder than it should be. Yesterday all we were trying to do was drive back to the bloody rental house. It should take an hour and a half from Blenheim, but no, the residents' convoy through the road construction is randomly not happening, and with no warning you end up stuck in Ward for six hours, and the whole trip takes about ten hours. We lost a whole day yesterday. And I hate this road. You feel like you can't rely on anything. I hope that will get better once the road is actually up and running again. But at the moment, even if you're feeling emotionally on top of things, on a practical level it's still a nightmare.

Anne Marie and I also talk a lot about the stage of life we're in, and how that makes a difference. You know, we're getting older—and I'm aware that this is a lot harder for some people, like the farmers—but really, we're too old to start again from scratch. It's so difficult to know where to go next, or what to do, or where to live, how to rebuild your life. It's so daunting. On the one hand I know we need to pick ourselves up and dust ourselves off. But on the other I just can't imagine never having Clarence times again. It was such a unique situation, and that was so much to do with the beautiful location, and the river. Where would we find somewhere like that again?

I always think about that. And now, the earthquake has changed the whole geography of the place so much that the river isn't even there anymore. Now it's just a big swampy lake. Even if we could rebuild the house in the same spot, it wouldn't be the same.

That's kind of helpful, in a way. It's just a different place . . . I've got to stop romanticising it, because it's gone now. I always imagine standing in the garden and looking out over the river, but even if I went back I couldn't do that now. I worry that I'll never be able to recreate that. I suppose we can't worry about that right now.

Well, that brings us neatly up to the present moment! The question everyone wants an answer to: how will we do it?

The perfect conclusion to your book: 'What the fuck will we do now?' But really, that is the question we're left with. And it affects everyone. Like, I know you're all grown up and you can get on with your own lives. But the fabric of your life is all unravelled, and no one really knows where they belong or how they belong until we can make that happen again.

But even when we got back to our rental house yesterday, after all the driving, it still felt like home.

Yeah, it was the same relief that it always is. I still felt, 'Oh great, I can get back and water the plants and do all the things that in the back of my mind I've been worrying about.'

It was a very specific experience for you—as a mother, as a 'housewife', for want of a better word—because the house was very much yours. It was your project.

I do think it was different for me than for all of you. You know, I'm there all the time. And truly, my greatest joy was that house and the home we'd built there. I know other people might think that's not very worthy, but I love doing that. I loved nothing more than the moments I would look around and see any of you or all of you at home, just doing what you do and having this space to belong to. That gives me so much pleasure. I used to worry, after the quake—and I have got over this a bit now—but I was honestly sick with worry that it would somehow mean the end of all our home time together, the end of our family closeness. It seemed so obvious that Matt, for example, would choose to go and stay at his girlfriend's lovely home rather than the two of them coming to stay in whatever random house we would be in. This was before we moved into our rental, I think.

I remember you getting upset about that. You kept saying, 'It's all over, it's all over.'

Yes. I mean, how embarrassing! But at the time it was this absolute fear that things would change. I don't feel like that anymore—I can see you're all adopting our rental house now, and that it is able to fulfil the same things. But it's not in the same way, because it's not our place.

In answer to your question, I do think it's harder for me. Dad can go off and get so absorbed in work, but really the home is my kingdom, and I'm proud of that. It does feel like a deep loss, and I just loved that garden. It made me feel so close to my own mum, and I really miss that.

Brave

It is 4am Sunday. I've been on call since Friday morning, but also had my parents staying which has, at last, brought me someone I trust enough to tell how I feel, and someone who believes and understands the sadness, frustration and despair Esther feels watching me disintegrate like an ultra slow motion car crash.

Woke earlier in panic and sweat after nightmare that started with me at a conference trying to sort out rural funding or something, ending in argument, then leaving that and becoming a race to find tickets and get to train platform to get home but losing Rufus and running back and forth in increasing panic till I woke up.

Have suddenly had a moment of clarity.

I know five very highly regarded rural GPs, my age or a bit older (four of whom have also been publicly acknowledged for their efforts, making my award feel like kiss of death).

All 5 left their practices in the last few years, only one had a nice planned retirement with the thanks and praise they deserved, and even then only just.

Final straw moments were:
- *marriage breakdown*
- *mental health issues*

- *'burnout'*
- *heart attack (attributed very much to stress)*
- *HDC investigation—so unfair and demoralising he resigned*

Any and all of those scenarios could be me right now.

Esther stands heroically beside me, but my life is consumed by work or feeling stressed by work and our relationship (and mine with the kids) teeter on the brink. I have no close friends.

As we have discussed I feel overwhelmed, anxious and depressed. I can see no way out of my work responsibilities and pressures, and no way forward from the emotional and financial disaster of the house we can't even visit, let alone use, rent, repair or ever sell; our most crucial emotional pillar and only financial asset is lost.

I can't give up with work entirely—I need to weather this storm and hope to return one day if I am ever to have a business that is worth anything.

I am in the worst physical shape of my life: high BP, massive stress, heart pounding as I write this, my head hurts, my knees hurt, I'm 10 kg overweight. I can't sleep and have a really awful sense of impending doom re health.

I am so behind with admin, results, letters etc. and so busy covering and advising locums, the newer doctors and the nurses that it impossible to stay on top of it all or even to know or remember what I have checked off or who I've seen. Mistakes are happening—two recent 'missed' diagnoses, complaints re late referrals etc.—I'm scared that I don't even know about what else I have missed.

Add to that a tolerance of zero and irritability—in the last few weeks I have made an embarrassing furious outburst at conference and have lost my temper with admin staff, a poor night nurse at hospital and patients. I am really worried about medicolegal risk and inevitable complaints that will grind on for years.

236

On Friday I had call about a long-time patient of mine who I had sent down to Christchurch earlier in week with what we thought was easily treated tumour; however turns out to be inoperable and essentially untreatable so I was told that she was coming back to 'GP care'.

I am ashamed to admit that my first thought was about how would I find the time, energy or interest for the horrible journey ahead, without a flicker of compassion.

I am not sure I can pull myself together for my acute clinic at 10am, or for the day and night on call ahead, let alone the next few weeks or months. I was thinking in mad desperation last night of ringing John Kirwan or David Meates to say please help me, what can I do? I cannot go on.

I am frightened; I don't know which of the outcomes will get me first, but feel certain this will not end well.

*

Dad wrote this letter in April 2017, a week before he was due to fly to Auckland and receive a New Zealand Bravery Medal for his service during the Christchurch earthquake.

Nearly six years had passed since the 2011 November earthquake, and yet somehow it seemed closer than ever, swelling up like an old injury, a long-suppressed grief making itself known. My elderly grandparents had flown 12,000 miles to be with us for the bravery ceremony. They had crossed oceans, my grandfather wheeled through airports and between gates, and had arrived, blinking, into an unfamiliar timezone, an overcast Christchurch day. Seeing his parents seemed to have broken something in my father; the child in him leaned into them, collapsing, wanting to be held.

Brave. The word felt simultaneously emotionally loaded and meaningless. 'I'm not brave,' he kept saying, defeated, despite our assertions that he was. In the days before the ceremony he seemed lost and deeply sad, messages flooding in from friends and family coming at him distorted and wordless, as though he was hearing them through a body of water.

It wasn't just the earthquake stuff. He was physically unwell, exhausted—wincing in pain every time he sat down or stood up, pale and sick-looking. The last few months were the worst I had ever seen him, his usual exhaustion making way for something more like total collapse. Mum had called me twice over the summer, crying and convinced he was going have a heart attack. There wasn't a question of him having time off—there simply weren't enough doctors around. And besides, everyone at his practice was working themselves to the bone; Dad was no anomaly.

Once, that summer, he called an ambulance because he was experiencing heart palpitations. He rang up my mother in a panic, but by the time he made it to the hospital his heart had calmed down, and he was back at work within the hour. We found it hard not to be angry with him—to accept, as he seemed to, that there was no system in place supporting overworked doctors and nurses. Dad was about to be recognised as a national hero, but all we wanted was for him to stop.

*

He showed us the letter in the morning. My mother read it, then my grandparents and then I did, all of us crying with relief to see him finally acknowledge what the rest of us had known for so long. He sent the letter only to Jo, the friend who had texted him, warning of burnout, after the Kaikōura earthquake.

He agreed that he had finally reached the point of burnout, and would now need to take time off work, regardless of the financial fallout. It had, in our eyes, become a matter of life and death; he said that he wasn't suicidal, but no one questioned whether or not he needed to be asked.

He called it 'giving up', and the guilt and shame he felt staggered me. The fact that he, a medical professional, a person who was supposed to be at the forefront of our mental health crisis, could have such a hard time saying the words out loud, was shocking and heartbreaking. We told him, over and over again, that there was no shame in what he was feeling. We were his team, the people who were proud of him no matter how he felt, who were always on his side. Even at the time, I felt painfully aware of how lucky we were. It goes without saying that so many others don't have access to the same emotional support, that not every family can afford to go two weeks with no paycheck.

He viewed his own vulnerability as weakness and failure. Here was my father, a proudly emotional man, a doctor, someone who had counselled other people through their own depression. And still, those words, so impossible to him. *I am struggling. I need help.* He stopped wanting to go into town or see anyone. If we were at the supermarket he wanted to wait in the car, to avoid the well-meaning people who would ask why he wasn't at work. I couldn't help but look around our small town and think about what other emotional undercurrents were running through it—farmers, tradies, fishermen. If Dad couldn't talk openly about his feelings with his medical colleagues, how would these other men be getting on?

He saw it himself only when his work announced to their staff that he was taking time off to sort out our broken home in Clarence. They were trying to protect him, but dismissing his mental health made him angry. 'Why can't they just say it?' he wondered aloud to us. 'Why can no one tell the truth?'

My mother—who saw my father's letter as a green light, the okay for her to spring into action—set herself upon the mountain of paperwork that she hoped would trigger his income insurance, something she had previously organised out of sheer fear for this exact situation. Proving that my father was mentally unfit for work was a lengthy and exhaustive process: counsellor and psychiatric appointments, boxes to be ticked and signed and processed. I laughed when Mum called me, overjoyed that the counsellor had diagnosed my father with depression, anxiety, survivor's guilt and post-traumatic stress disorder. 'She told me he's in absolutely no state to work,' she said, thrilled. And then, 'Why are you laughing at me?'

Dad was given three months off, and while we cheered when he came home after his last day, we knew that it would be a long road to recovery, and that none of his problems would go away overnight.

We can make a life

When I talked to Dad about writing this book, we discussed how he would feel when people read it. It wouldn't be quite the same as Adam Dudding's *My Father's Island*—a memoir I had recently read—because the author's father had passed away some years ago. His story was reflective; his father wasn't around, afterwards, to have awkward encounters with people in the supermarket, to have strangers feel as though they knew his story.

My father is a private person. His assertion in the letter that he has 'no close friends' isn't true, but the sentiment—that he doesn't easily relax around people outside his family—is a real one. I was surprised, in our conversations about this book, to find him so keen for me to begin, and so eager to share his story with me. I worried he was agreeing to this project out of love for me, and that in writing it I would be adding to his burden.

Dad has always supported my writing, welling up at almost anything I put in front of him. When I was accepted into the Master's in Creative Writing, Dad was the first person I called. He whooped down the phone at me, so proud and so excited, calling me back a few hours later to go over it all again.

My siblings and I love to make him proud—in some ways,

wins of our own feel like an easy way for us to help him, to cheer him up. Once, I was invited to be the guest speaker at an event at my old high school. The speech went well, and afterwards I overheard Dad say to my mother, 'At least I know I've done one thing right in my life.' At the time I laughed at how overdramatic that was, but underneath I was relieved, and pleased.

In my conversations with Dad about this book, we also found ourselves talking over and over again about mental health. It was such an easy phrase to throw around, but in real life it remained so hard to make sense of. We tried to talk objectively about his feelings of shame, and the response he'd had when he'd finally voiced them. We talked about the difficulties faced by rural doctors, many of whom he knows and admires. We talked about how, after writing his letter, all Dad had wanted to do was to 'send it to the press'—to show people that this was how he was feeling. He wanted to be clear: this was how bad it was. Not just for him, but for so many others in his profession.

Over my year of writing, the severity of our mental health crisis is reiterated over and over again. In August, the number of people who have taken their own lives by suicide reaches the highest annual figure ever recorded. In October, new research shows that one in three secondary school students self-harm. I can see it all around me: flatmates struggling with depression and anxiety, people posting on Facebook about friends they've lost to suicide. All the while, people I run into tell me they've seen Dad on the news, or they comment on his Bravery Medal. What a hero, they say, what a legend.

When I think about this book, I worry that I'm somehow telling it wrong, that it's too much, that in twenty-five years I'll regret my emotional, underedited writing—but all of it still feels true for me. As well, some fundamental—maybe idealistic—part of me believes in the power of sharing stories, in the importance of being personal and vulnerable.

A few weeks ago I was visiting home, and my parents and I drove down from Kaikōura to Christchurch for the day. We had lunch at an Italian place, and as we sat around the table conversation turned to my uncle Andrew, one of their greatest friends, the man who had brought them together. In the last year he had been diagnosed with an aggressive frontotemporal dementia, a rare disease which attacks the parts of the brain that control decision-making, behaviour, emotion and language. He's in his early fifties, his youngest daughter seven years old. Although his diagnosis neatly explains years of increasingly strange, sometimes disturbing behaviour, its finality is devastating, and my parents are heartbroken. His illness has progressed so much that, in my last conversation with his immediate family members, they described what felt like a death without dying, an adored father and husband completely lost to them although he still sat beside them at the dinner table.

While we ate, my father began recounting a sailing story, one of many that involved him and Andrew facing wild waves, some unbelievable twist or escalation that always made us laugh or shake our heads in disbelief. A phrase caught my attention as he talked. 'What's a following sea?' I asked.

'Oh,' he said, 'it's when the waves are heading in the same direction as the boat. Which is fine when the waves are manageable—you just move along with them—but if they get bigger, or faster, they can get a bit overwhelming. They can knock you off-course or capsize the boat, if they're wild enough.'

When I thought about it later it seemed like a perfect metaphor. Life pushes you along, all steady and fair sailing, and then out of nowhere the wind picks up. The waves, when they come, are like the trains that used to rocket past our Hāpuku house—fast, unstoppable, thundering along and leaving a bright stillness in their wake, a noisy quiet.

As the year draws to a close, I meet my publisher and editor in their offices in Kelburn. I sent them all my work in November: hundreds of pages, a year of writing. A large part of me still can't believe they have said yes—that, incredibly, all this work will be something physical, something I can hold in my hands. 'How shall I finish it?' I want to know, having sent them a chaotic manuscript with no ending. I wasn't sure how to wrap up a story that was still unfolding. When I thought about my family it felt like we were still only just surfacing—out of this particular wave, perhaps, but still treading water, exhausted.

They reassure me that, actually, this is something good about my story, that it's a moment in time, that I can write up to as far as we've got and leave it open-ended, as it is in life. Later that afternoon, when I call my parents to recount the details of the meeting, my dad takes this open-ending to mean that he needs to do something dramatic, to present me with the final chapter by way of bold decision. For example, he suggests, perhaps we could all move to somewhere more interesting, like Nicaragua. That would be a good ending, wouldn't it?

'No!' my mother and I say in firm unison, rolling our eyes. 'That is not what that means!'

*

Later, lying across my bed in Mt Cook, I listen to an interview with the writer Arundhati Roy. I read her book *The God of Small Things* when I was at high school. It became one of a handful of novels that I would repeatedly return to, hoping to recapture the feeling from the first time I read it, the bone-deep discovery of what words could do.

In the interview, Roy talks about her mother. As a child she can remember her mother singing a love song called 'Hi-Lili, Hi-Lo'. Roy grew up in a village in Kerala, the same village in which her book was set. Her mother was beautiful and headstrong, and before Roy was born had rebelled against the traditional Syrian Christian community she belonged to by marrying a Bengali Hindu. When they later divorced, she returned to a village where 'she was not wanted, with her two children who were even less wanted'.

'I think when I was even three years old,' Roy says, 'I might have been a writer then, because it was hard to be that young and to understand why an adult who was harsh with you was being harsh because her own heart was broken, you know? Children shouldn't understand those things, but writer children probably do. She used to sing this song and I'd listen to it and think, oh, this woman is beautiful, and she's young, and it's over—in terms of love.'

The song was from *Years Apart*, by Martin Taylor's Spirit of Django. It's a sad song, of lost love. I am surprised to find myself crying, with Roy's lilting voice in my ears. It's such a specific kind of pain, the knowledge that your parents are suffering. 'Even now,' Roy says, 'it harms me to think about it.' She pauses. 'But we don't walk away from harm.'

*

Now it's nearly Christmas, thirteen months since we lived in Clarence. This time last year we were on the family holiday that we so nearly abandoned: three weeks of sunshine in the far north, postponing thinking about what waited for us back home. Every morning the boys went out in the boat, hunting ever-elusive kingfish with their spearguns. They arrived back each afternoon deflated and empty-handed—until Christmas day, when they went out early and turned up, hours later, holding two 18 kg fish above their heads, each over a metre long. Their shouts of excitement were audible even before we saw the boat appear, and Mum, Hebe and I cheered from the beach at the sight of them.

This Christmas we'll be in Kaikōura. Only a couple of

weeks ago, Rocky messaged me in Wellington to tell me that Mum was in the garden again. She'd finally rescued her pots from Clarence, and now she was outside, planting things.

Kaikōura is a beautiful place to be this time of year. When I come home, Mum and I get coffee sitting across the road from the ocean, the mountains sweeping sharply down into the sea. The movie theatre, when we drive past, is fenced up, still with faded posters advertising films that came out a year ago.

Dad is in great spirits—excited to have all five kids back for summer, sitting round the table with the boys, mapping out fishing spots, drawing up plans for a speargun rack to attach to the boat. He looks better, too, less of a shell, his face tanned from all the biking he's been doing. I need him to read my writing, to make sure he's okay with it all, but I'm worried it will stir things up again, bring him down. It's been nine months since he wrote that letter, when he was probably the lowest I've ever seen him. When he eventually reads it back, he is shocked. 'Did I write this?' he asks incredulously, looking up at Mum and me. 'Bloody hell. It's miserable!'

'Yes,' we say. 'It is. But you were, too.'

*

We are planning Ruf's twenty-first birthday party, a long-awaited event happening in the middle of January. He has a lot of ideas for how twenty-firsts should be, having been to a fair few. He seems to have more friends than any of us—you can't walk through the supermarket without him shouting 'G'day, mate!' across the aisles, slapping hands with the tradies, fielding banter from just about everyone. Our friends think he's hilarious—they'll call him up just to say hello, send him postcards from their overseas holidays. When he's visiting Christchurch with us, a stream of people pick him up and take him off to barbecues, or rugby games. He's in his element when he's at the pub shouting rounds for the boys, doing everything in his power to avoid Mum, Dad and his siblings, who might attempt to control his beverage consumption. A few of our close mates joke that they know they've got to the next stage of friendship with Rufus when they are similarly avoided at parties, close enough with him to know when he's getting carried away and needs an earful. 'Remember when Ruf used to think it was cool to hang out me with me?' Matt's friend Ben laughs when we're at a bar one afternoon in Christchurch, Rufus ignoring us from across the room, where some friends of friends are cracking up while he puts on a show. 'Hot chicks, hot chips,' you can hear him saying. 'That's my motto.'

For his twenty-first he only has a few requests: two marquees, a live band and a party bus. We roll our eyes, asking him where exactly he's planning to get the party bus to take him and how he thinks we'll get one to Kaikōura. But we're excited, too—I can't wait to stand up and tell him that he's nailed his twenty-one years, that he couldn't have done it better if he'd tried. Messages pour in from friends and family. We have to turn people away who are asking to make speeches—it seems like everyone has a funny story to tell.

Finn, Matt, Rocky and I want to organise something extra for him, something that will make him laugh and feel loved. Maybe, we think, we could arrange a haka for him, his way of expressing the intensity of emotion he feels when we're all together. But it could be hard to organise, and we wouldn't want it to come off messy. He loves music—Kenny Rodgers, the Black Eyed Peas and Adele all incite in him impressive dance routines, eyes squeezed shut with emotion at the high notes. Maybe we could do a performance for him, to one of his favourite tunes.

Rocky picks it in the end, the perfect song. Rufus always plays it in the car when we're driving, or when we're playing music round the dinner table. It's Fly My Pretties, the song 'We Can Make a Life'. When it comes down to it, all my brothers will happily get up in front of their friends, dance a little, embarrass themselves. We kind of owe it to Rufus for all the times he's pulled us out of sadness: a funny line, a stupid expression or a 'Rufus tuck-up', coming into our rooms at night and pulling the duvet up to our chins.

The song is a live recording from the Fly My Pretties album *Live at Bats*. The band sing the lyrics line by line, and then the audience sings them back until everyone has learnt the words and can sing it together. It's a simple song, and Ruf—not usually one to worry if his lyrics don't even slightly resemble the actual lyrics of what he's trying to sing—can always get these ones exactly right.

'*We can make a life, we can make a life, we can make a life worth living.*'

Acknowledgements

To the people who supported this book back when it was still just an idea, my unbelievably generous Boosted donors—thank you. You gifted me the two best things, time and space, and this book wouldn't have had such a smooth journey into the world without you. To my classmates of 2016, who made me feel safe to grow, and who taught me so many things about writing (and life in general!)—thank you for your friendship. To Ingrid, Pip, Emily and Elizabeth—I came back to your words so often as I wrote this. I am the luckiest to have been taught by you.

To Penguin New Zealand, many thanks for your permission to quote the passage on page 131, from Patricia Grace's *Cousins* (1992), and which can be found on the Wellington Writers' Walk. To Judith Huntsman, thank you for your direction regarding the Tokelau chapter—your help was so appreciated. To Mike Ardagh and David Galler, thank you for your invaluable advice and knowledge regarding the medical aspects of this book.

To Granny, my long-time penpal, thank you for all our conversations! To Olwyn and John—for the sleepovers, maths lessons and constant encouragement, thank you. To Lucy, for always cheering me on, and to all the Hones—

thanks for letting me write about our girl.

To Bop, for your early read, and for climbing to the top of a hill to get signal so you could call and tell me what you thought. Thanks for all the tireless work you do revolutionising the way we treat and talk about mental health. You're doing so much good, and I'm proud to know you.

To Oli, for important title research! To Claire and Lily— thanks for always making me feel totally at home, and for being so excited about this book with me. To Ethan, for late night wines and such a solid friendship. To Tom, who understands me so well.

To Harry, who gave me so many confidence pep-talks. Thank you for always listening and loving. Your kindness is my favourite thing about you.

To my incredible female friends—especially Hannah, Rosie, Issie, Albie, Laura and Jackie, whom I lived with while I wrote this book—thank you. I truly couldn't have asked for a more inspiring group of women to share my life with. I absolutely love you!

To the people of Christchurch and Kaikōura, especially to those who were connected to the tragic events at the CTV building. I hope that by telling my own personal story, you feel in some way that yours is acknowledged too.

To VUP—I'm still buzzing that I got to share this experience with you. Thanks Fergus, for your confidence in the 'me' parts, and for backing this book when it had such a long way to go. Thanks Kirsten, and thanks especially to Holly, who once called a new paragraph 'badass' (the greatest compliment ever) and to whom I am forever indebted for editing this book so beautifully.

Thank you, most of all, to my family. To Finn, Matty, Rufus and Rocky—you guys are my support system, and I'd be utterly lost without you.

To my Mum, who read this first. I am forever proud and in awe of you. Thanks for being such a fierce defender of the things that are important, and for trusting me with your stories. You keep me steady.

Lastly, thank you Dad, for sharing so much of yourself with me. I know there are people out there who will read this book and feel less alone because of you. Thanks for leading by example, for being brave in every sense of the word. Some part of me will always be in India, sitting at the Shore Bar with you.